OLD AUNTS
&
AUNTS

n ISABELLA ELIZA LUCIA Minnie John

Wilfred   Tennant CHRISTINA EVELYN GERTRUDE
  m   m
Catherine   Gladys×

× brother and sister

THE AUNTS

THE AUNTS

Mora Dickson

THE SAINT ANDREW PRESS
EDINBURGH

First published in 1981 by
The Saint Andrew Press
121 George Street, Edinburgh
Copyright © Mora Dickson 1981
ISBN 0 7152 0491 2

Printed in Great Britain
by Thomson Litho, East Kilbride
Bound by Hunter Foulis, Ltd.
Edinburgh

CONTENTS

For my cousins,
and all in the next generation who
remember the aunts

1

The Family

'William, Isabella, Eliza, Lucia, Minnie, Tina, Lillias, Cassie, Jenty, Mary, Agnes, John.' So my mother used to reel off her Paterson mother's family. It was a party trick to see whether she could still remember them and we listened with delight, ready to catch her out. In her ninety-seventh year she could go through the list without hesitating though almost everything else, including the names of her own grandchildren, had been forgotten. She must, however, have got the order muddled, for Agnes, who was born in 1847, was the third daughter—and Helen, the oldest child, who died of whooping cough aged two, was never mentioned.

Because the great-uncles had faded away long before we came on the scene it was the great-aunts who gave this roll of names reality for us. In truth some of them were dead too; nevertheless they retained a corporate identity with those still living. Of all the

ten daughters only two married, Cassie, and Agnes, who became
my grandmother.

When we began to climb the close stairs to visit the Glasgow
flat where four old ladies kept house together the unitary nature
of the Old Aunts was firmly established in our minds. That
Isabella and Lucia lived independently made little difference to
our view of them as somehow on extended leave from this family
enclave. Perhaps the fact that I never remember visiting Old
Aunt Lucia in her own home and knew Old Aunt Isabella, who
lived in England, only through letters, helped to connect them
with the one setting I could visualise as being appropriate for Old
Aunts. In the flat itself there were memories and mementoes of
the dead sisters—photographs, delicately painted china—which
combined with our knowledge of their place in the family hierarchy to make their physical absence seem more fortuitous than
permanent.

We had aunts of our own too, with a roll call equally illustrious,
for my mother was one of Agnes and Alexander Sloan's thirteen
children: Norman, Thomas, William, Alexander, Edith, Nancy,
Lillias, Mora, Wilfrid, Tennant, Christina, Evelyn, Gertrude.
Once again, though the uncles married, only two of the seven
girls found husbands; Nancy, who trained as a doctor, and Mora,
who was my mother.

The family was Glasgow born and bred; part and parcel of that
great dark dirty city which was also my birthplace. But, although
they belonged there and that was their setting, our own aunts
were not town people. They might live in surroundings which
overawed young country relatives but their talk was often of
Highland walks, long bicycle rides, picnics beside fishing lochs or
disasters on hill golf courses. Grandfather, though since being
born in Bridgeton in 1843 he had never lived or worked anywhere
other than Glasgow, was a formidable outdoor man. The children and their mother spent long summer months in the country,
where he joined them at weekends; on less protracted holidays

both he and they, sometimes separately but often together, headed for the nearest rivers and hills.

Perhaps my grandmother was less addicted to country living, though her father too had spent much time with his family outside the city. But the choice of holiday house, in the days when Granny was burdened with babies and complicated domestic arrangements, seemed often to have been made more to suit Grandfather's love of fishing and walking, and the energetic pursuits of his older offspring, than to provide temporary relief from the pressures of daily life for his wife. Isolated in remote rural spots, there was sometimes not even a village within a distance to which she and the babies could reasonably walk. And she feared horse transport. One of the often repeated stories which regaled our youth was of her birthday treat. It fell in August, and Grandfather invariably celebrated it by hiring a waggonette to take the whole brood on a monster picnic—to the terror of poor Granny who spent the day in an agony of anxiety lest the horses should bolt and precipitate waggonette, passengers, food, drink, fishing rods, babies and all the paraphernalia of a day's outing into the nearest ditch. She travelled crouched down behind the coachman, so that her view of the road and its possible hazards was totally obscured, and prayed for the day to be safely over. Though her daughters may have sensed her unhappiness, it never seems to have made the slightest difference to the form taken by this yearly diversion.

Agnes Paterson and Alexander Sloan were married in 1870 and then 'entered upon fifty-three years of unbroken happiness', to quote Grandfather's words after she died, written to his youngest daughter. It was true that they were, and remained, devoted; nevertheless Granny had not had an easy time. They had lived together forty-four years when she wrote to one of her sons, on the occasion of his own engagement, 'The girls say to people "Mother does not believe in marriage" but that is not the case.' My mother also told me this, though she did not add what a cousin said *her* mother had passed on—that Granny had urged one of her daughters to be sure to have a baby, even if she did not marry!

Looking back on her life, Agnes Sloan explained to this greatly loved son the tribulations which, in spite of her love for her husband, had resulted in the repressed, rebellious sadness misconstrued by her daughters. For twenty years, in indifferent health, she had produced the babies whom she adored; and for the next twenty had striven to rear them and keep the large household going. Grandfather was strong, active and constantly out of the house, engaged in business, taking part in many Christian and philanthropic activities around the city, or cycling, fishing, walking, golfing. 'A man takes for granted that a woman should always be at home,' Granny wrote. 'I had many disappointments, often being unable to leave home even to enjoy myself . . . it was a sore struggle many a time.'

Now, however, with her grown-up children round her and Grandfather 'as much, if not more, fond of me than ever', she felt that she was reaping her reward, and admonished her son to remember in his turn that women needed love and sympathy.

The family that Granny and Grandfather brought up was, and remained, close-knit; strongly conscious of its own identity and generating an internal vitality which ensured that the members found an endless fascination and interest in each other's doings. It was the girls who exemplified those characteristics, rather than the handsome, hard-working, self-effacing brothers. Each parent gave credit to the other for the continuing strength and affection of family life, but while Granny passed on to her sons the quiet constancy and devotion that had brought her through so many trials it was, perhaps paradoxically, not from their mother with her tribe of unmarried sisters but from Grandfather that his daughters inherited their self-confidence and zest.

He was a man of the utmost probity, admired and respected in the business circles in which his work lay, with deep religious principles which, as a matter of course, he put into everyday practice. Warm-hearted, with a robust capacity to enjoy energetic pursuits, he was fond of children and took a constant pleasure in the company of his own. Both individually and en masse he loved them, not perhaps with demonstrative affection but in a more potent manner, showing a continuing interest in their development, taking it for granted that whenever possible they would join him in the things that he liked to do.

So it came about that the reminiscences of a happy childhood, with which we were entertained by our mother, were spun round the stocky moustached figure of Grandfather striding out over the hills forgetting that his legs were sturdier than those behind, skating with abandon, or cycling blithely along the Loch Lomond road with sons and daughters in attendance. Grandfather loved fishing, golfing, skating, curling, swimming and diving—but above all he was a mighty walker. Till the day of his death at the age of eighty-four he walked through the Glasgow streets to and from his office in the city.

Sports and outdoor pursuits were a major preoccupation within the family, even though female offspring predominated; though curiously Grandfather greatly hurt the one son who gained international eminence in rugby football by showing no interest in his achievement. My mother, very close in age to two younger brothers, spent much time wishing that she had been born a boy and longing to forsake for trousers the unwieldy, earth-sweeping skirts of her youth. The aunts spoke of their father with admiration and anecdotes. A note of pity entered their voices when their mother was mentioned.

But to Grandfather, Agnes was all that he had ever desired. He had proposed to her by letter in September 1867 when she was twenty, 'fortune not having favoured me with a fitting opportunity of declaring my love' during the summer holiday, and married her three years later. In the manner of his time he may have been insensitive to the burdens under which she sometimes faltered, but he never ceased to love and admire her for the next fifty-three years of their lives together. She bore the children to whom they were both devoted, in her case particularly to the 'beloved sons' four of whom arrived in the same number of years after their marriage. Two she had to watch die in their youth, one she let go to a lifework in India, though it cost her a great sacrifice, and in her old age another did not return from the Great War. She ran the big impractical house, bulging from cellars to attics with children and servants, and managed to feed, clothe, keep warm and happy this assorted tribe until her oldest daughter was able, quietly and efficiently, to take over some of the responsibility. All this she did on a modest income, made for her that much more of a restraint because Grandfather was strict about money and she dreaded asking him for the weekly housekeeping. She was not without a quiet sense of humour, commenting when her first granddaughter was born that the baby looked like herself—'so she will do.'

There may have been strains and tensions with so large a family, but Agnes Sloan never regretted having any one of her babies. In her old age she recorded her thankfulness for so many children and for holding the love of them all. In her seventy-sixth year she came up to the drawing room after supper one evening, settled herself in her chair by the fire and quietly died.

I was five when this happened and my impression of her was of a withdrawn, somewhat forbidding, figure in black. For me the one vital link between us was her attempt to dissuade my mother from giving me the family name of Agnes. Her own daughter christened by that name was always known as Nancy. She did not succeed, but I could not help feeling that we must have shared a common detestation of it, a conviction that warmed my memory of her.

It was, however, Sloan, not Paterson, exuberance that survived in Agnes' daughters.

The known ramifications of the Sloan clan were many and various, extending to second and third cousins—and others even more remote whose provenance was hazy but whose identity was firmly established as 'our relations'. There were black Sloans and red Sloans, the former good, the latter bad. It may be that some on Grandmother's side crept in to this great cloud of kinsmen, but so strongly was the Sloan stamp set upon us that we took it for granted that they were, or had become, members of that prolific family. Listening to the stories of the aunts' youth it sometimes seemed that there had been little need to know anyone else, and certainly the outsiders, whether ultimately they had joined the family or not, glowed infinitely less vivid on the family canvas.

There was a curious paradox in that failure to achieve the unassuming decorum at which the Sloan sisters all aimed. 'Now don't make yourself conspicuous,' my mother used to admonish me before every occasion on which I might possibly come into the public eye—whether it was a dancing class, a Christmas party or, later on, simply going out for a meal with a friend. It was a caution with which, I feel certain, Granny also used to guide her daughters. To me it seemed to have been a lost cause. Each of the sisters possessed an innate, if unwanted, capacity for conspicuousness, and taken together it would have been hard indeed to ignore them.

On the other hand they were jealous that they should be recognised for who they were, not from personal pride but because the achievements of any one of them reflected credit on the family as a whole. When my first book came out, many years after my mother had relinquished her maiden name, she said to me in an absent-minded moment, 'But you haven't put your real name on it. How will people know you are a Sloan?'—forgetting that even my unmarried name had never been the same as her own.

My brothers and I stood in a double relationship to this formidable clan. Brother and sister had married brother and sister, thus in some measure drawing into the same orbit our immediate patriarchal relations. This meant that even one of our two non-Sloan aunts had, confusingly, the surname Sloan; and our only cousin on that side of the family was also, as we were, half a Sloan.

In a real sense we were the country cousins. In our small town when my mother said, 'Remember who you are', she was not exhorting me to live up to my Sloan heritage but referring to our local family reputation. Nevertheless, especially as I grew older, my yardstick of acceptable social behaviour was often a mental reference to the aunts and their likely reaction in the event of a public revelation. By a curious chance my first passionate kiss took place outside their front door. A budding relationship which never recovered from my simultaneous surmises about what the sleeping aunts on the other side of it would say did they know what was going on.

Perhaps because we rarely saw them casually—met out shopping or arriving unexpectedly for tea—the aunts had a special aura in our eyes. That, and the fact that we knew so much about them. Not that our meetings were in any way formal, far from it as a rule, but distance demanded that they be planned ahead in some detail, and my mother's well-known propensity for making arrangements, both in advance of any undertaking and while engaged in it—in the latter case as insurance against catastrophe—made certain that we were all keyed-up in expectation for some days beforehand.

We did not go to Glasgow lightly then, and for this reason it was necessary to put together an intricate jigsaw of essential things that must be done. The centrepiece was the visit to the aunts; the framework in which it was set included a number of imponderables. The car, to be got ready so that there should be no breaking down on the bleak moor uplands; good weather, to be prayed for especially in the fog laden atmosphere of the town; decisions about time of departure, and the agitation of preparation so that we should all be ready at least half an hour early.

Those days stood out in our calendar, particularly when we were small and outings to any city few and far between. Nor were they always anticipated with enjoyment, for a regular component of the jigsaw puzzle was a visit to the dentist. This we viewed with a horror that never eased, causing our hearts to sink as we stepped into the car and our stomachs to churn when the countryside gave way to the first town streets. He was the aunts' dentist too, but his familiarity with our family history in no way altered our view of him as a cold-hearted monster.

Fortunately his appointments were usually first on the list, so that the subsequent meeting with the aunts found us in a state of euphoric release from fear and prepared to do our bit in the give and take of conversation.

It may be that for the aunts too, because they saw less of us than the other nieces and nephews, those occasions assumed a rather special air. They were prepared to give us all their attention, taking an interest in our doings, never brushing us aside as too young to be heard once we had been seen.

Though being heard, however much our contribution might have been welcomed, was often an impossibility. Joined by my mother, whom they had not been with for some weeks, both sides pregnant with family news and excited by the chance of telling it to a fresh audience, the sisters fell into an orgy of intimate communication whose decibel level rose continuously until the eardrums rang with it. All were incident-prone, prepared for life to present them with minor adventures—which it constantly did. Each was capable of delivering a dramatic monologue with flair and feeling. In sisterly conclave, perfectly in tune with every shade of audience reaction, this art flowered. With only the children as observers, and inhibitions about exhibitionism thrown to the winds, a crescendo of interruptions, screams and laughter echoed round the room as each aunt in turn—and the full orchestra of aunts together—played with a sure touch on the instrument of family understanding. In the arguments that invariably developed each aunt had a definitive view which brooked no check from the others and each held to it whatever evidence was presented to the contrary. 'Sloan women always know best,' their nephews by marriage used to say—with a sidelong glance at their own wives.

There were two aspects to our perception of the aunts. Individually we recognised how much they differed from each other, and this very diversity allowed the nieces and nephews the luxury of special attachments which might change over the years as one's own interests and inclinations altered. Such particular links were rarely openly acknowledged, for the corporate body of aunts was scrupulously fair in its love and favours. Looking back I wonder whether they vied with each other for our affections. If so it was not apparent to our unsophisticated eyes, though once or twice I was aware of undercurrents in the continuing struggle to maintain the delicate balance between personal identity and sisterly cohesion. One niece was later asked not to write communal letters addressed to 'My dear Aunts', as they preferred to hear from her separately.

Within the home they had roles, based on seniority—though aptitude played a part also. In the latter case, domestically, it was less the use of an enjoyable skill than an excuse to hand over some unwelcome task; in the former the exercise of authority, though willingly conceded, was jealously guarded. Outside the house each had her own sphere in which she could, if she so wished, live without reference to the others.

The group identity had peculiar characteristics and took its colour from the core of three sisters left in a house of their own after the death of their father. There they might occasionally be reinforced by two more, one on leave from a missionary hospital in India, the other looking after a brother's motherless family a few streets away. In time both those aunts joined the other three, merging, it seemed easily, into the corporate body. In reality it cannot have been such a simple transition for either of them.

In contrast to the Old Aunts, who wore black and lived in the aura of a bygone Victorian age, the aunts gave an impression of colour and vitality. And height. It was not until I myself was nearly grown-up that I realised with a shock that most of the aunts were of middle size and two of them quite small. Somehow personality combined with a multifaceted image produced an impression of large physical presence. When the door opened, and aunts emerged from various parts of the house to greet us, it was like being enveloped in the voluble, dark-eyed, roman-nosed warmth of one hydra-headed aunt whose benevolent intentions were never in doubt—but whose many-armed attentions could be intimidating.

They seemed, and remained for many years, ageless. It did not occur to us that any of them were, or had even been, young. Indeed we were not altogether wrong in thinking them middle-aged, for my mother was thirty-six before I was born and by the time I was five years old the youngest aunt must have been in her thirties. But, though I speculated about many things, the age of the aunts was not one of them. They had passed through the time when they might expect the years to bring those alterations naturally connected with the heyday of life—or so it seemed to my uncomprehending eyes—and entered upon an endless fea-tureless plain, where even the seasons stood still and the milestones, the fears and the crises of the outside community failed to register. To have perceived change in them or recog-nised that the group, as opposed to the individuals who com-posed it, suffered from the same human uncertainties and failings as everyone else we knew would have shaken the foundations of my world.

Besides we all knew about their youth. Since we were small we had heard the family history told and retold. We enjoyed our mother's presentations of moments of high drama and tolerated the reminiscences so constantly sparked off by incidents in our own lives. We had listened, sometimes because we could not avoid it but more often enthralled, as early recollections were jogged by the communal auntly memory. The matter of hus-bands, or lack of them and a connection with the Great War, did not wholly accord with a hint of vanished suitors attached to two of the younger aunts. In that there *was* room for speculation. But all this was in the past. A part of history, like Queen Victoria's funeral when my mother had been twenty and remembered the countrywide sense of shock, or the first motor car. Those things had happened before we were born and, while they gave the aunts a satisfactory solidity as actors in a serial whose highlights we knew by heart, now it was our life that was in progress; theirs had stopped.

But it had not come to a halt in the past. They were very much part of my present and it was to be a long time before I had any sense of leaving them behind. Ageless they might be, outdated they were certainly not. The portion of my spirit which was sensitive to their unconscious influence was considerably less inhibited than that which feared the judgments of my mother. The multiple persona of the aunts stretched a sympathetic umbrella over many quirks of character and behaviour that within the closer unit of my family I feared might not be condoned. Aunt Chrissie, after all, was always making herself conspicuous; and it did not require any great stretch of imagination to picture Aunt Evelyn as having known what it was to kiss a young man on a doorstep.

The ability to remain securely based in my present was a remarkable one. They had been born in the reign of Queen Victoria, and were in their thirties before women got the vote. Their youth had been spent encumbered by ankle-length skirts and elaborate constricting underwear. My mother used to talk with scornful horror of red flannel petticoats, though I suspect that those garments were apocryphal in her own family. They had seen the transition from horse to motor car, and come to accept the responsibility for domestic duties that even a family of modest means had once been able to delegate to two or three servants. They had watched their close warm world broken open by a major war, after which the past acquired a nostalgic hue. At a period when social custom greatly restricted the life of any woman unsupported by a male of her own, when they had seen the hopes of such an attachment gradually fade, they had chosen the reality that belied the conventional myth. Not for them the fainting fit and the chaise longue. They went out and became involved in the many activities of their city which without the work of single women would have left the community infinitely poorer. The backward looks were full of gratitude and laughter, and quite without self-pity. To me they never seemed to doubt that they were fortunate.

Then too, although they had not married, their lives had never been without men. They were reared in a household where common sense and the ability to hold their own in robust familial competition was more valued than helpless femininity. Though some, my mother among them, suffered from poor health in the fog-ridden miasma of Glasgow winters, and Agnes, my grand-mother, feared for their lives and resorted to cocooning remedies, nevertheless they grew up with a brisk disregard of personal ailments and a scorn of coddling. Accustomed to a father who saw no need to keep them confined, and brothers in whose active lives they played, whenever possible, an equal part, living within the orbit of cousins and nephews, they were never deprived of male company. Whatever the secret longings of their hearts for something more far-reaching and profound than this general dispensation, they had an understanding of masculine companionship and interests which more sheltered young women lacked. They did not live a life noticeably deprived.

My mother became engaged to be married on a Sunday. When Grandmother was told she was shocked at such a use of the Sabbath and hoped that somehow this momentous event could be returned to store until Monday. 'Oh Mora,' she said, 'Could he not have waited?' A somewhat dampening response to such an announcement. My mother and her sisters, on the contrary, saw every justification for happiness and the Lord's Day going together. 'The better the day, the better the deed,' my mother had replied, refusing to keep secret her acceptance of the proposal. It was not that the engagement came as a surprise to

Granny, for she had feared weeks before that the family alloca-
tion of telephone calls would soon run out if Mora continued to
ring her young man as she seemed to have begun. She also noted
that her daughter had been extremely critical of a brother using
up the phone calls to the same purpose the autumn before and
remarked, tartly, of the new situation, 'We shall see how that
goes on.' But she held strong views about subjects suitable for
Sabbath contemplation.

Though there might be differing ideas as to the daily applica-
tion of their faith, there was no doubt in any of the children's
minds about the Christian beliefs on which family life was based.
Every morning Grandfather started the day off on the right foot.
Several small grandsons were left with an indelible picture of the
huge sombre dining room, with three chairs set out at one end for
the maids, aunts disposed round the table and on the sofa, while
Grandfather led them all, as he had done every day of his married
life, in a Bible reading and prayer. Granny may have favoured a
more rigid interpretation, but Grandfather's Christianity was
joyous and contagious. It sprang from a profound knowledge that
the nourishing source of life was spiritual and lay in a personal
relationship with a living Saviour. Good works might be the
outcome of this conviction, but to maintain that they could
replace it was a heresy. So his daughters worked quietly among
the poor and desolate, but they too recognised that this was the
result of a living trust in God and not a substitute for it.

Growing up in an atmosphere where adults and children
alike—not only in their own large family but within the wider
extended clan of cousins and relations—held common beliefs
and values to be important made for stability and cohesion, and a
view of life in which each had an honoured and worthwhile place.
There was no immunity from tragedy, heartache, disillusion,
disappointment, but their Christianity provided an immense
reservoir of spiritual strength on which to draw to meet those
times of human unhappiness.

My mother had a love-hate relationship with her native city, which did not seem to have spread to her sisters. Having escaped to a country life, she looked back on aspects of the town with a shudder. She never heard a true Glasgow accent without making a face of distaste, and to be likened to a 'Glesca keelie' indicated considerable disapproval of our appearance or behaviour. The dirt, the damp fog-ridden winters, the echoing close mouths hauntingly lit by flickering gas jets, up whose oozing stairways she climbed to visit a crippled girl or a member of her Guildry Company, the weight of wet bedraggled skirts, the rattling, shaking tramcars, assumed Dickensian proportions in our demonology. 'The clartier the cosier'—the dirtier the more comfortable—a phrase used about the sewing of Gorbals children into their clothes at the beginning of winter, was common in our family as a joking excuse for rather less drastic evasions of the opposite maxim about cleanliness and godliness.

All the Sloans detested strong drink, a facet of evangelical Christianity reinforced by the appalling problem of drunkenness in the streets of Glasgow. The teetotal prohibition was accepted as sensible and rational and never enforced by moral preaching. Only as we grew up, among contemporaries who found this a peculiar and constricting rule of life, did the offer of a glass of sherry become another act the response to which was mentally measured, with some anguish, against a standard set by the aunts.

That conditions in Glasgow were Dickensian there is no doubt. But the warmth, vitality and humanity flowing out from the great evangelical meetings at the Tent Hall, with their rousing Moody and Sankey hymns and choruses, counteracted the more oppressive physical features. In her own way each of the sisters tried to combat the squalor and misery of which they were well aware, through church work, Sunday School, YWCA, nursing; but they knew too the exuberant communal pleasures of a day's outing 'doon the watter' from the Broomielaw, concerts in the public parks and later the Orpheus Choir, the superb Art Galleries, circuses, open-air meetings and winter skating, all enhancing urban life. For the aunts, memory was softened by continuing familiarity with the constant growth and renewal of the city.

The house in Crown Circus, associated with the aunts in our early memories, had been for many years the family home. It stood on a rise, facing down a slope, its height exaggerated by this approach. The blackened exterior and the steps up to the front door, under which the basement lurked, added to an intimidating external appearance. The atmosphere of informal jollity, which was an essential part of the aunts' later home, was absent from Crown Circus—though the welcome was no less warm. Each time she saw it afresh my mother would shake her head over discrepancies between the carefree, well-fed, happy memories of her youth and the impossible difficulties of running such an unwieldy house which her own experience had now taught her to recognise, and murmur, 'Poor dear Mother. I don't know how she did it.' For her part, after her daughter's wedding, Granny had written, 'It must be queer for her to have plenty after always being accustomed to a very poor purse.'

Inside, the setting was dark and red, with heavy furniture. A central staircase connected its many storeys. Aunt Edith, herself dark and often dressed in shades of red, presided over the household with quiet efficiency. Perhaps it was seeing her coming down those stairs in neat, straight, high-necked clothes that created a lasting impression of tallness. Only when I myself became a gangling, overgrown teenager did I discover to my astonishment that she had seemingly shrunk to less than my own measurements.

When my oldest brother was six or seven he had his tonsils out. This fearful operation, which we all in turn had to undergo, took place in Crown Circus, memory says on the landing on a well-scrubbed kitchen table, though the vast dining room with its enormous family board seems a more likely venue. Afterwards he convalesced surrounded by aunts consoling him with curds and jellies.

The drawing room, on the first floor, was L-shaped, flooded through long narrow windows with whatever light the day afforded. Round the corner from the door was Grandfather's seat beside a bright fire of Highland logs culled from a summer holiday. If he was at home Grandfather might well be working on a rug, having taken up this occupation after an attack of shingles when he was eighty-three. But this did not mean that he was housebound and inactive. On the contrary, he continued to go daily to his office, often on foot, until his death a year later.

Grandfather loved his small granddaughters—as he had loved and cherished his daughters. Though grandsons predominated, it was the infant achievements of the little girls that he mentioned often in letters. 'Grandfather's gate' in the park was so christened by one of them because she and her mother often met him there prepared to be amazed and delighted by the latest accomplishments.

He was a handsome, vigorous, kindly old man, and it must have been painful to him emotionally—though it was never so physically—that in the last few years of his life he developed a gross swelling on one side of his face from which his young descendants instinctively shrank. Concentrated X-ray treatment made no difference and the fear that the growth might be cancerous prevented surgical exploration. Never a vain man, he continued to live an active life among friends and colleagues ignoring the burden of such a conspicuous disfigurement.

In the winter of 1927 the lump began to discharge and in a few weeks it had disappeared, so that at the very end of his life Grandfather reverted to his normal good looks. It was not for long. One day in his eighty-fifth year, Aunt Evelyn walking along a street in town saw a stretcher case being carried out of the Central Hotel, where Grandfather had been attending an official lunch. She did not know until she arrived home that the casualty had been her own father, struck down as he would have wished in the midst of a still busy life.

Ten years later, after considerable difficulties in finding what all
the aunts could agree on as a possible home, Crown Circus was
sold and the aunts set up a new residence in Bute Gardens.

The dining room in both houses was dominated by a portrait of
Grandfather presented to him by the Institute of Accountants, of
which body he had been Secretary for thirty-six years. As was the
custom they commissioned also a picture of Granny and that, as
he would have wished, hung beside his. They were large official
pictures, created for boardroom or office, and out of all propor-
tion to the small new house. But Grandfather's painted face, with
its bright interested eyes and white hair and moustache, was
sympathetically portrayed and it was love, not filial duty, that
hung it where his daughters ate, literally, in its shadow.

The house at Crown Circus had been tall and black. Bute
Gardens was very different, though it too stood on a hill, above
the university on one side with the Byres Road and the Botanic
Gardens on the other. It was a low, two-storey, terrace house of
red sandstone, with a flat roof. Struggling valiantly with the
Glasgow soot, a small garden behind and a border in front were
tended with more or less success depending on which aunts were
in residence. The core members of the group, who left home only
for holidays, were Aunt Edith and Aunt Lillias, the two oldest. But
daffodils bloomed bravely in front, and at the back it was really
only possible to see the garden if specially invited to do so—often
when a cherished root of primrose or heather had been brought
back from some expedition and still retained sufficient memory
of its native air to flower.

The doorbell sounded loudly, but rarely brought an immediate
response. Then a curtain would twitch in the dining room bow
window and high pitched cries began to echo and re-echo
through the house, as though the aunts were checking up on that
day's door-opening rota. When at last the lock rattled and the
door drew back we would see aunts, alerted, emerging from
every corner of their home.

The top landing at Bute Gardens was curiously designed with a large open square space, entered by a door, round which lay a warren of aunts' rooms. Nothing much except the storage of the sewing machine, the ironing board, old tin trunks from the travels of younger aunts and mysterious items concealed by exotic materials, velvet and old brocade, seemed to happen in this central void. It was ill-lit, with an impersonal shadowy mustiness made cryptic by the bordering closed doors.

The aunts' rooms were sacrosanct, not for casual display to prying eyes. One entered only if invited, and this was a rare and special honour. For my part Aunt Chrissie's was the only one with which I was at all familiar, and this was because we shared a talent for painting. For the others, I do not remember seeing the inside of Aunt Edith's room until she was dying—and by that time I was grown-up. In those rooms the aunts lived their personal lives. Here they could be as ascetic or flamboyant as they chose, indulge in a fondness for walls cluttered with prints and post-cards, or cupboards bulging with unworn clothes; they could be meticulous or sluttish as the mood took them. No one questioned, however long or short the hours, what they did there. In those tiny kingdoms they were their own mistresses.

Downstairs, except for one bedroom beside the front door, they lived communally, conscious of the niceties of age and seniority, anxious to mitigate—or conceal—signs of friction or disagreement. Being, all of them, strong-minded women, differences of opinion were frequent and, in our view, entertaining. Dates and personalities in the family history were the subject of many arguments; and their concentration on our pleasure could lead to competition in gauging our tastes in food and entertainment. They were not slow to let each other know that we had been given too much or not enough, or might prefer to do this or that. Lunch in the dining room, under Grandfather's painted eye, occasionally resulted in lively discussion when aunts who had not been in on the secret discovered what lay beneath the lids of serving dishes on the sideboard. We ate it whether we liked it or not, but we were aware that there was not a unanimous front on food, as there was at home, and that some of the aunts felt much the same as we did about the frogs' eyes in sago pudding or the slippery nothingness of curds and whey.

Tea in the small drawing room, full of family photographs and knick-knacks, with Aunt Edith sitting on the left of the fire, the silver teapot by the window presided over by the youngest aunt, cakes and sandwiches on a spidery tiered cakestand and Aunt Lillias always in a hat, would start with some little formality and end in a riotous reunion. Somewhere in the house in those early days a little servant lurked, doing her best to keep an eye on Aunt Edith in moments of conflicting domestic messages. As times grew harder she changed to a daily until at last the aunts themselves did battle with the kitchen range and the intricacies of a complicated feeding pattern.

Entertainment could take varying forms, individual aunts sometimes suggesting expeditions tailor-made for one particular niece or nephew. Aunt Chrissie took me round the Art Galleries, expatiating with elegant gestures of her long-fingered hands on the beauties of pictures she especially admired while I stood beside her in tongue-tied silence, awed both by my own ignorance of a subject in which I was passionately interested and by her exuberant and extremely conspicuous exposition. When we were smaller the aunts enjoyed playing Halma and Spillikins with us. Sometimes we all went to the circus in the Kelvin Hall, where spectacular transformation scenes flooded the ring with water. For my older brother they devised the very satisfactory solution of giving him the fare for a full round on the Subway, which he could board at the station down the hill in the Byres Road. But they professed themselves shocked when, much later, another nephew, newly engaged to be married, brought his own entertainment and sat down to embroider dinner mats for his future home—an unmanly occupation in the aunts' view.

When we left Bute Gardens to face the long journey home in summer twilight or bitter winter darkness, it was always to a rousing farewell of shouted last-minute admonitions and messages, interspersed by uninhibited laughter. The aunts did not giggle; there was nothing refined or respectable about their mirth. If they enjoyed a joke they saw no reason, conspicuousness apart, why their amusement should not be plain to everyone. Ricocheting from one to the other, reinforced by appreciation as it went along, laughter whizzed round the little hall and spilled out into the street. Sometimes it was we, wary and anxious, burdened by the cares of adolescence, who seemed to have reversed the natural order of the generations.

As the door shut behind them we left with the feeling that all was well in the aunts' world.

2

Aunt Edith

It was Aunt Edith who held the keys and took charge of the communal housekeeping purse. The oldest girl, she had been eighteen when her brother Tom died of tuberculosis at the age of twenty-two. For Grandmother, after the death of fourteen-year-old Willie in 1887, it was the second loss of a dearly loved son in seven years and she was stricken to the heart. But life had to go on in the busy household, where the youngest girl was just three; there were still seven school age children and one of the other daughters had an affected lung. Without fuss Aunt Edith began to relieve her mother of much of the burden of housekeeping. Long before Granny died it was Aunt Edith's hand that held the reins, firmly if unobtrusively; when Grandfather was left alone Aunt Edith cherished and looked after him, and to the end of her life hers was the authority that all the sisters recognised. In 1919 she herself had a critical illness from which she nearly died and the family began to wonder what they would do without her.

She had always been plain, with a long, rather equine face, a large mouth and straight thin hair scraped back in a bun. Her dark eyes were watchful and kind. This strong cast of feature was inherited from Agnes Paterson, though one of the younger aunts liked to suggest that the family Roman nose came from the Duke of Wellington. How this had happened was never gone into.

Aunt Edith's style of dress was severe, only a tendency towards rich reds indicating a nature no less eager and passionate than her outwardly more flamboyant sisters. She indeed did carry with her an aura of an older generation. Her clothes, high-necked blouses with a brooch, flat brimmed hats, would have seemed out of date—except that they so perfectly fitted her looks and character.

Aunt Edith was Miss Sloan, a much prized distinction as through the years, inherited by death, it fell upon one after another. Every other female of that surname in the connection, aunts and nieces alike, had to be content with an initial placed before it. To me there was always something inexpressibly grand in this pre-eminence, and I used to be glad that there was only one contender on my father's side standing between me and the undisputed right to use my own surname without the identifying initial.

At first sight Aunt Edith could look forbidding in the eyes of her young relatives. Less demonstrative than the others, she waited quietly in the background while greetings surged round the group and the first excitement of meeting was expended. But she was neither inconspicuous nor unnoticed. That we eventually found ourselves sorted out, and any urgent need that we might have hesitated to express catered for, was due to her quiet competence. She was in charge and we never doubted it.

But this first impression of austere detachment was quickly dissipated. Aunt Edith had not only been an elder daughter, she had helped to bring up hordes of younger brothers and sisters, some still in their teens when the first nephews and nieces began to arrive, and she had never lost the gift of sympathetic insight.

When a young niece, whose parents were in India, came to live in Crown Circus it was to Aunt Edith that she gave her confidence, finding her not only trustworthy but also fun. It was true that few concessions were made to a child in the house. Aunt Edith saw that she made her own bed, helped to lay the table and undertook other simple household chores, not taking it for granted that these things were for others to do. She could come home from school to find precious possessions given away to the less fortunate, without permission sought or granted. But such things were an accepted part of childhood, and there was never a moment when Aunt Edith did not make it plain that she was there by right as a member of the family—and welcome. For Aunt Edith herself, at this time fifty-three, there may have been a return to the pleasures, as well as the responsibilities, of bringing up younger relatives. Certainly, although she was the oldest of the aunts, her niece found her the least critical or fussy, the aunt to whom in a crisis she would instinctively turn.

Aunt Edith had in her day been a good golfer and an elegant skater, as we well knew, and those past achievements gave her status in our eyes. It was not difficult to imagine her gliding over the ice in the wake of Grandfather's precisely cut figures of eight, and in my mind's eye the flat brimmed hat, high-necked blouse and flowing skirts attained a visual grace in that setting which they never succeeded in doing in reality.

The fervent involvement of the Sloan sisters in the life of their own family, of which we were willy-nilly a part, made it impossible for us to regard them as one-dimensional figures. Though we often, and uproariously, played a card game called Old Maid, I do not remember that we ever associated that sad figure of fun with any of the aunts. There was an element of loneliness and rejection attached to it that was quite out of keeping with their full and lively lives.

Aunt Edith could talk to and entertain the young. When a joke appealed to her sense of humour or she became caught up in the re-telling of an incident, she had an unexpectedly deep and irresistible laugh, bursting out, loud and jolly, more than holding its own with the others. Then her dark eyes sparkled, her sallow face broke up into hearty wrinkles as she gave way to her enjoyment.

She had some musical talent and could play and sing. A lifetime's devotion to Sunday Schools, as both practical teacher and administrator, had given her an easy familiarity with the kind of melodies that appealed to the young. More mundanely, she would sing nursery rhymes for small nephews, accompanying herself with great verve on the piano. Indeed, once seated on the stool, she cast off her natural gravitas and flung herself into the tune in hand, her playing, like her laughter, refusing to be confined by any notions of sentimental understatement.

Born into an age of home-created entertainment, she had her party pieces—which regrettably we mimicked unmercifully when well away from her presence. A favourite for this exercise was Robert Burns' 'Ae fond kiss, and then we sever! Ae fareweel, alas, for ever!', a song of intense gloom to which she summoned all her talents of voice and expression with full-throated passion. Exaggerating wildly, heads flung back, music sheets trembling in our hands, our voices rocketing from bass to high contralto, we found our imitations excruciatingly funny. In a sense Aunt Edith herself when she sang seemed a caricature of the aunt we knew, and it was perhaps the discrepancy between her normal behaviour and the glimpse of unsuspected exotic depths which caused us to exorcise some personal uneasiness in this particular way.

Accepting the doctrine of inconspicuousness, the great Christmas gatherings at which we were all expected to perform caused me much secret anguish. I knew then that, whatever my physique might pretend, the Sloan blood which ran in my veins had been considerably diluted. I could never, as the aunts seemed able to do when in the bosom of the family, fling off all inhibitions and give joyous rein to whatever gifts I might perhaps have inherited.

On July 21st 1926 Grandfather wrote to his youngest daughter, 'This is Edith's jubilee birthday. Isn't it appalling!!! She wears well, dear girl, and has made good use of her years.' Indeed she had, quietly, without fuss, in the great tradition of Christian and philanthropic endeavour which gave scope to the talents, abilities and justifiable ambitions of thousands of women who would otherwise have been restricted to a narrow domestic circle. It has become fashionable to deride the efforts of those valiant women and to question their motives. What is rarely conceded is that much of the work undertaken by Aunt Edith and others like her laid the foundations on which was built our own welfare state.

Aunt Edith was content to labour where there seemed to her to be a need. She used to sing a chorus, 'Jesus bids us shine with a clear pure light, like a little candle burning in the night' which ended '. . . and so we must shine, you in your small corner and I in mine.' This faithfully described her attitude, even though her own corner had enlarged itself until it covered a considerable field.

She was a good organiser and administrator, serving on many committees, her common sense and lack of personal ambition helping, as it did at home, to resolve differences and keep the peace. But, as with her nieces and nephews, this did not mean that she held aloof from involvement with people. There were many young women in distress, mothers in despair with intractable family circumstances, wives, or indeed husbands, with complex marital problems, who turned to Miss Sloan. She never failed them, having in abundance the most valuable of all gifts, the willingness to listen and the heart to take endless trouble on their behalf.

We were aware of this activity—in the background of our lives though in the forefront of hers. We knew of arrangements for great missionary meetings in which she was heavily involved. We had seen her return home tired, often wet, from a journey across the city to the dock areas to fulfil a commitment, on the kind of day when it would have been infinitely preferable to stay indoors. We had been at Bute Gardens when the doorbell rang and a request—never refused—came in to see Miss Sloan. But she did not expound to us on this side of her life, though she did not conceal it. When we were present Aunt Edith was at our disposal, interested in the things we were doing, prepared in the most natural way to step into our world.

She had a specially soft spot for her nephews. Of the first five children she had been the only girl and perhaps this gave her a particular understanding where small boys were concerned. It may well have been too that, when our family went to visit, my brothers offered a welcome variation in a company in which my mother and I were two more females among so many. Not that there was ever any sense of discrimination, but instinct told me that she had a special affection for my older brother—who reciprocated it—while she delighted in the irreverent camaraderie with which my two younger brothers often treated her.

Though she was known to have had at least one offer Aunt Edith was never associated in my mind with any long-vanished marriage chances. She must have been thirty-eight at the start of the Great War which, rightly or wrongly, we thought the cause of the lifelong single status of her younger sisters. Looking back it now seems to me that Aunt Edith, moving early into responsibility for a large household, the confidante of her father, accustomed to the companionship of brothers and sharing common interests with them, may have found herself in a situation which there was little urgency to alter. Some of the frustrations which beset junior aunts were absent in her case. As Aunt Chrissie was to say later, 'The trouble was that coming from a family of fine brothers no other man ever matched up', and there may have been some truth in this.

In large families, with a strong core of solidarity, married relations take adequate care of the matter of direct descendants. Grandfather was not likely to lack grandsons and granddaughters whether Aunt Edith added to their number or not. If there is no personal desire to leave a living mark on posterity, in such a situation there is no pressure on those who lack a maternal urge to produce children. Besides there are satisfactions of a different, though no less potent, order in the role of aunt and great-aunt. Aunt Edith was heir to a powerful tradition in her own living aunts—born in the first half of the nineteenth century—and could look forward through her growing nieces to stretching out a hand into the latter half of the twentieth. Though patriarchal by structure, it was the women who held this family's bonds together, who nourished the roots of the tree and through whom the memories and stories were handed down that kept it living. In this process Aunt Edith held an honoured place.

Gothic in repose, in the strong lines of feature and dress; when animated suffused with warmth and fun; unchanging in a hazardous and fearful world, at the unquestioned, though never indulgent, disposal of heedless nieces and nephews, Aunt Edith was the archetypal aunt, seemingly different in essence from the other four who bore openly with us a greater share of the ups and downs of the human condition.

3

The Old Aunts

That the Old Aunts were also the aunts of our aunts never occurred to us. We saw ourselves as being the centre of the web of relatives and it was, on the whole, their relationship to us that mattered, not to each other. The endless intricacies of degree in distant cousins, whether once, twice or three times removed, had ourselves as the reference point.

Besides, in the case of the two sets of aunts, one group was ageless, the other ancient—a gulf so enormous as to make ludicrous the idea of only a generation separating them. Aunt Edith, with her strong Paterson features and a hint of the nineteenth century in her clothes, formed the only possible link.

In memory the ceremonial visits to have tea with the Old Aunts always took place when the weather was dismal, the Glasgow streets wreathed in wisps of yellow fog and the trace horses, standing waiting for their next burden at the foot of slippery cobbled hills, hung their heads wearily and puffed gouts of steaming breath through great red nostrils, or buried their faces in damp nosebags while the harness clanked and a great hoof pawed at the roadway, striking sudden sparks from it.

In actual fact the sun must sometimes have been shining, though always finding it difficult to penetrate the Old Aunts' physical surroundings.

They lived in Kersland Street, itself cobbled and sloping, bordered by tall, blind, black tenements built in stone. We left the raucous tramcar at the bottom, listening to the bell as it clattered away taking normal life with it, and then climbed the hill rather slowly wondering what on earth, when the moment came, we were actually going to say.

The close mouth was impersonal and desolate. As we entered it the temperature dropped several degrees. The stone stairs were hard underfoot and our voices echoed up the empty well. We took our time, feeling the next hour a weight upon our chests.

On the first floor the door, thick and dark, was as forbidding as all the rest. We waited outside while our mother spruced us up and the bell tinkled faintly in the distance. There was a strong smell of cats, a sound of footsteps, then the door was flung open and Bridget stood on the threshold.

Bridget was very Irish, quite without a sense of deference, and most of us were frightened of her —though it was true that one set of cousins, whose father had Irish connections, actually seemed to like her. She had been with the Old Aunts a long time. A fringe of unkempt grey hair straggled under her cap. Her white apron was not quite clean. She was reputed, when alone in her tiny kitchen, to indulge herself with cold porridge and this greatly enhanced her oddity. Bridget confined to cold porridge because the Old Aunts were impoverished, or because they saw no reason why she should have it hot we could have understood. But it was a matter of preference. She actually liked it that way and this to us, who had ambivalent feelings even about hot porridge, made her a very peculiar creature indeed.

She greeted us, in a strong Irish voice, with a familiarity that we were quite incapable of returning and did not know how to cope with. It was impossible not be enveloped in her frowsty presence. In the small dark hall she took our garments and ushered us into the overcrowded sitting room with a breezy announcement. Her whole attitude was at variance with the painful awe with which we stepped forward to greet the Old Aunts, and it did nothing to ease our sense of disorientation. Having satisfied her own curiosity and been recalled to her duty by Old Aunt Eliza, Bridget then disappeared back into her kitchen to get the tea.

She had four old ladies under her devoted, if somewhat haphazard, care. Three of them seemed incredibly antique, clad in long black skirts with high-necked blouses and a shawl to keep out the cold. Above this sombre garb a wrinkled yellow face inclined in our direction for a scratchy, hairy kiss. The fourth, Old Aunt Eliza, very upright and regal, with a dash of purple or puce somewhere in her garments, held court beside the fire.

Though too intimidated to ask any questions, we knew that they had what I considered a romantic past. In the 1715 rising the Paterson family had been compromised and lost the ownership of their land. A century later, in 1811, my great-grandfather was ten months old when his father died leaving a widow in poor circumstances to bring up eight sons and a daughter.

Thomas Lucas Paterson proved to have a talent for getting on in the world, and an equal facility for losing—not always through his own errors—the gains that he had so painfully won. In the depression of 1842, two years after his marriage, the business that he had built up failed. Undeterred he started again, doing sufficiently well to be able to take his wife to a meeting of the Anti-Corn Law League in London in 1846. On this occasion the mail coach horses took fright some twenty-five miles south of Glasgow and ran away furiously until stopped about three miles further on, by a steep hill rather than an impotent coachman.

Maybe their daughter Agnes's fear of horses was the result of her mother's tales of this alarming incident.

In 1851 Thomas Lucas Paterson again took his wife to London, to visit the Great Exhibition, and over the years of the Old Aunts' youth, though he continued to have intermittent financial difficulties, the family lived in some style with two daughters at school in Brighton and one in Cheltenham, visits to Malvern for the cure of various ailments, long summers in houses in the Scottish Borders.

In October 1878 the City of Glasgow Bank failed and with it went Thomas Lucas Paterson's credit and livelihood. For some years he attempted to retrieve his lost fortune, but at last he was left barely able to exist on a legacy belonging to his wife. His unmarried daughters found themselves unexpectedly forced to earn their living.

This scenario followed closely that of a number of books that I wept over in secret, and the parallel with fiction, at that time my window on the world, made the Old Aunts real and interesting people in my eyes. It also gave me a profound fear of bankruptcy, because I could not imagine what I would be able to do in such circumstances. I gazed at the examples of dead Old Aunt Lillias'—or was it Old Aunt Minnie's—china painting in the flat and wondered if they represented a contribution to the family finances and whether I was capable of doing the same.

Old Aunt Eliza had become a governess when catastrophe struck and she carried with her still a pedagogic air. It was she who issued the invitations to tea and organised the event, taking care to see that entertainment was provided for the children—a three dimensional stereoscope in which we had the fascination of seeing prepared views come alive. Improbably Old Aunt Eliza gardened, in a tiny sooty square at the back of the close, no doubt with memories, of which we never dreamed, of more spacious policies in days gone by. It was she who was occasionally encountered by Glasgow based nieces and nephews—or even perhaps by my brother en route to his solitary Subway rides—

shopping in the Byres Road, her face with its Roman nose proudly erect, shrewd old eyes alert for a relative or a bargain. If anyone coped with Bridget she did; she decided what sandwiches we would have at tea.

While Old Aunt Eliza talked with our mother we were despatched round to do our duty by her sisters. They liked to savour us one by one, which greatly increased the strain on our limited conversational powers. Invariably one was in bed; sometimes it seemed to me that two were, though this may have arisen through my inability to distinguish very clearly between Old Aunt Tina and Old Aunt Jenty.

Perched up on pillows in a narrow brass bed, her Bible beside her on a table, wrapped in a white shawl instead of a black one, a little head with thin hair scraped back emerging tortoiselike from the woollen carapace, Old Aunt Jenty—or Old Aunt Tina—lay waiting for a visit. When kissed this cheek was soft and papery and the voice that issued from the faded lips was very quiet, demanding a good deal of nervous concentration to understand what was being said.

But the image of immense and fragile old age rooted in a small anonymous bedroom conflicted with that other knowledge which, like Old Aunt Eliza's three-dimensional picture holder, bestowed a wavering life on the person before my eyes. Both Old Aunt Tina and Old Aunt Jenty had been missionaries in India and the oriental objects to be seen about the flat gave substance to what might otherwise have seemed an impossible claim. Indeed there were moments when the wizened olive face on the pillow looked not unlike a transposed Indian visage.

In the year that the City of Glasgow Bank failed, 1878, these two sisters had been appointed to India by the United Free Church of Scotland. It was to be another six years before Thomas Lucas Paterson finally lost his entire substance, and three more before Old Aunt Jenty, having served nine years, resigned and came home. But Old Aunt Tina, in charge first of the Christian Girls' Boarding School in Bombay, remained to create a lifework and to retire after thirty-three years, honoured and loved. In her quiet way she had pioneered among women whose lives were restricted or truncated by social custom, helping to found the first Christian Women Workers' Union and initiating industrial work for those widows whose husbands had died of the plague. In the zenanas of Bombay, where the feminine portion of the household lived in strict seclusion, both Old Aunt Jenty and Old Aunt Tina had been familiar figures. Did they, I wonder, in later years ever think of this flat as the zenana of Kersland Street?

Perhaps they talked to me sometimes about their experiences, forced by my shy silence to do so. It was not a totally strange world, for my mother's married sister, Aunt Nancy, had been a medical missionary in India, one of the earliest women in Glasgow to become a fully qualified doctor. And Aunt Gertrude, the youngest of the unmarried aunts, a trained nurse, had also offered her services in the mission field.

In our own home drawing room meetings were not unusual, addressed by tired missionaries from exotic places like China, Bolivia or Nepal. My father had travelled widely and had a heart open to every appeal. Listening to the guest talking in the evenings, recounting tales of strange places and of people with very different customs, I came to have a perception of the world as immense, uncomfortable—and dangerous.

The latter impression I kept secret. Mostly there was a hopeful gloss on anything I overheard. But physical appearance can belie verbal evidence, especially when accompanied by a yearning tenderness. When the missionary from the high Andes said goodbye his gaunt yellow face conveyed what no one would ever have told me, that he had struggled unceasingly, and perhaps unsuccessfully, with his vocation and was now going back to die. When, after a long silence, the news of his death eventually came to us I was not surprised.

But, deep down, I was alarmed. For the thought of being a missionary attracted me. It seemed to be one of the acceptable things to do, and the evidence of Old Aunt Tina and Old Aunt Jenty pointed to it being possible to be a missionary without being very clever. There were two snags however: I was an only girl and it was obviously easier to get away when you were one among many—and in my heart of hearts I was afraid.

Which added a certain fascination to the visits to those two Old Aunts. Lying in a high bed in a room crowded with furniture, how could one imagine such a frail little old lady ranging the immense, fiery open spaces of India, battling with disease, snakes and spiders, talking about her Christian faith to Indians, and accepting challenges which I knew myself to be incapable of facing? How had they lived to come home? Was it not even faintly disloyal to have done so? Between visits only the names survived, Jenty, Tina, somehow lilting and youthful; sitting beside them they represented an enigma.

On state occasions Old Aunt Mary rose from her couch to greet us. We never knew what she had done when crisis overtook her family, but a legend among her great-nieces whispered that she had retired to her bed to avoid the unpleasant consequences and then enjoyed ill-health. Whatever the truth, she did not seem to need a past to justify her existence. Old Aunt Mary was noisy, merry and totally deaf.

She sat in a low chair with a stool beside her, her nutcracker face split in a grin and an enormous tortoiseshell ear trumpet at the alert in one scrawny hand. Her own voice was like a cracked foghorn, dominating the room, relishing jokes after which the only laughter was often her own. She loved company, and neither age nor handicap was going to prevent her making the most of it.

In her youth Old Aunt Mary had been very gay. She spoke still of carriages and balls during her father's periods of affluence. Even among all the trappings of age and physical deterioration it was possible to catch a glimpse of the extrovert girl, much less given to serious things than some of her sisters. There was a rumour that it was Mary whom Grandfather had first courted, before he began to take a more sober view of life and turned to the less exuberant Agnes—leaving Mary to be content with the role of bridesmaid.

For us she was the real terror of the visit. We could just manage to cope with the two gentle ex-Indian Old Aunts, one of whom claimed without foundation that she was already one hundred, both of whom were content with our stilted replies to orthodox questions. Bedside sessions were the more easily endured from the knowledge that we would be rescued by a time limit. Old Aunt Eliza was forbidding and she could be sharp—but she had dealt with children in her day and she took the initiative in entertaining us.

But Old Aunt Mary was unpredictable—and determined to have her pound of flesh. Conversations with her went against all the canons of inconspicuousness. Of all her great-nieces and nephews only one was known to relish it, because her voice happened to be of a pitch that Old Aunt Mary never failed to hear.

Individually we sat on a small stool at her side. She grinned at us roguishly and picked up whichever hearing aid she thought suited her purpose. The trumpet she tried out when hoping to join in a general conversation: for more intimate talk there was a piece of flexible gas piping with a rubber plug at one end to fit into her ear and at the other a tin funnel, ordinarily used to pour liquid into a bottle or can. It is the trumpet, nevertheless, that I remember. It loomed enormous as Old Aunt Mary pointed the wide mouth at the nervous little face beside her. It was a cavern, inside which any sound that one might make would be diminished before it even left the daylight and wound its way up the narrowing darkness of the stem, at last to make contact with Old Aunt Mary's eardrum. Experience told me it was hopeless before I began to speak, but Old Aunt Mary had no mercy.

'Speak up. Speak up. What did you say? I can't hear you,' she would screech, thrusting the trumpet forward as though to push it down my throat. I could almost have put my whole head into it, and felt inclined to do so to hide the appalling embarrassment which covered my face with red.

But Old Aunt Mary was not appeased by signs of evident confusion. She wanted to talk to us and was not going to be denied her pleasure. The rest of the room had stopped to listen. Not that the interchange was riveting, but because it was difficult to concentrate on anything else while Old Aunt Mary's voice crackled through the atmosphere.

Despairing I raised my pitch as high as I could, overcome by the enormity of being the focus of attention. It was not only that I could not make her hear. I did not know what to say either. The timid observation with which I had started the encounter had become meaningless with repetition. Nor was the situation helped by the fact that I had ceased to be able to understand a word she was saying, though it seemed to have an enjoyable content for every now and then she gave a great cackle of laughter and the trumpet wavered in the air before my face. Sometimes, even, she would startle me by barking out, 'Don't shout. I'm not deaf,' when I was unaware that my voice had risen above a whisper. I fear she must have thought her great-niece a nitwit, a judgment which I would have had no difficulty in sharing with her.

Rescued at last by my mother, it was a relief to watch one of my brothers take my place. Though she still screamed at them to speak up they seemed to have more success than I did in establishing communication. Besides I had a suspicion that they rather enjoyed shouting. A cousin who was fond of telling the assembled company jokes was reported to have been ordered to stop by Old Aunt Eliza, herself convulsed by laughter, because she feared that Old Aunt Mary, driven frantic because she could not hear, waving the trumpet in the air before her like some anguished tentacle, might have a fit from frustration.

For the Glasgow-based young relatives there was the ritual ordeal of being summoned to tea with the Old Aunts on New Year's Day, and facing the outrage of Old Aunt Mary's personal remarks. One dumpy teenage great-niece was told that she looked like the mother of twelve. The oldest of our cousins, when she arrived at marriageable age, for a number of years suffered the embarrassment of having Old Aunt Mary's annual wishes piercingly broadcast to all and sundry. 'Well—a very good New Year to you and a husband before the end ot it!'

Old Aunt Mary was far gone before this event materialised, but when it did my cousin made every effort to get her to understand that an engagement was now an accomplished fact.

But, however terrifying the ordeal of talking to Old Aunt Mary, she was the one who left an indelible impression on her great-nieces and nephews, not simply of anxious confrontation but of an encounter with a character, a jaunty spirit battling to keep a hold on life and wanting, in spite of the difficulties which constantly thwarted such an ambition, to know something about us. Perhaps, after all, it was not only from their father's family that our aunts inherited their zest.

Old Aunt Mary lived, increasingly bedridden, until she was nearly ninety, into an age when more sophisticated hearing aids began to be developed. One after another they failed her and she returned to the trumpet and the old gas piping, pointing them at the world, demanding of them that they should continue to yield up to her the family information that she so much enjoyed.

There were two other Old Aunts who, although they did not live at Kersland Street, belonged to its ambience. This was particularly true because their own physical backgrounds were unknown to me.

Aunt Lucia had a house outside Glasgow. She too had gone off to be a governess and ended up running a hostel for fallen girls. She must have been a formidable warden and mentor. She was large and stout, with the carriage of a duchess—a phrase used about her by older relatives which irresistibly connected her with Tenniel's illustration to Alice in Wonderland. Aunt Lucia's face was pale and plump, with a feature that was the cause of considerable apprehension when one became the object of her attention. As a result of trouble in her youth she had a wall eye.

It was milkily white, deadening her right hand profile. When confronted full face the effect was eerily confusing. Where, and how, was she looking at one?

I was fascinated by this eye. It drew me to scrutinise it whenever possible. I could not decide whether its influence was baleful or benign. Did it hurt her? Could she really see nothing out of it, or was the blue veined whiteness merely a veil behind which the eye continued to take secret stock of all around its owner?

Our meetings with Old Aunt Lucia were usually at family gatherings when, before her arrival, her garments were a source of speculation to all present. She loved clothes, a trait which she transmitted to at least one of her nieces. She was not an extravagant spender; there was no money for that, but over the course of a long life she can have thrown very little away. Not for Old Aunt Lucia the annual clearance for the jumble sale or the indigent gentlewomen which so infuriated me when, at a later stage, I came home from school to find a favourite jumper ruthlessly discarded without my consent.

Aunt Lucia's wardrobe ran the whole gamut of costume from mid-nineteenth century to mid-twentieth. She was not content with the black skirts and plain blouses of her three housebound sisters. She rang the changes on satin, velvet, lace, chiffon and georgette; pinchbeck and jet, cameo and coral. What black there was, to set off the mauve, cerise or plum, was in a different league from Old Aunt Mary's woollen shawl and heavy serge. Draped, flounced, gathered, cunningly held together with a Victorian pin and adorned by chains, necklets, endless chinking bracelets and a velvet neckband, Old Aunt Lucia's gowns were a triumph of artistry. Taken apart, and laid out for inspection by a critical eye, they were no doubt a collection of odds and ends, often rusty from old age or misshapen from adaptation. But arranged upon her large frame and carried off by her commanding presence, crowned by the mystery of the wall eye, her dresses assumed a magnificence that none of her younger relatives, whatever their fortunes, could ever have hoped to match.

Old Aunt Lucia ate a great deal. There were those in the family who said that she was greedy—though I do not think we were meant to hear that. Now I wonder if, without the ministrations of Bridget, she fed herself properly when alone. Her gargantuan appetite on communal occasions may partly have been an insurance against the lean days, though there was no doubt that she enjoyed her food.

The unseen Old Aunt, who nevertheless haunted my life, was Isabella. She lived on the south coast of England, in itself an exotically improbable place to make a home. Perhaps when the crash came she had returned to make a living to the town where she had scholastic connections. It is probable that she was estranged from her sisters for I do not remember that her name was ever mentioned in Kersland Street.

How these old ladies existed materially was a mystery, for their father had been able to make little provision for them and, valiant though their own efforts had been, it was impossible to believe that they had earned enough to sustain their longevity. Pride and independence they had in abundance; pensions did not exist.

But family solidarity was a bulwark against outrageous fortune. My grandfather was very good to his sisters-in-law, and his son in turn accepted the responsibility. Once a year, when on a business visit south, he went to see Old Aunt Isabella.

She was not grateful—they none of them were, resenting his careful stewardship, unable to accept that their patrimony was not greater than he allowed it to be. Small, grumpy, isolated from her sisters—though never apparently considering that she might return to her native city—Old Aunt Isabella grumbled unendingly about the burdens of life. But for her too the family link, however tenuous, remained important. When I was about eight or nine she began to write to me.

For several years the fat envelopes, sometimes correctly addressed, occasionally, with a lapse that even then I understood, to Miss Mora Sloan, were handed over by the postman. Inside the spiky, uneven handwriting covered many pages. We had few reference points in common, and what she wrote was often incomprehensible to me, but I replied in short, stilted notes, proud in some obscure way of this correspondence. Perhaps the desire to have an unshared Old Aunt of my own played its part, for I imagined, wrongly as I later knew, that she wrote to none of her other great-nieces, and I enjoyed the feeling of being singled out. There was a tendency in my family to consider those letters from the south coast as tiresome and senile. I thought them extraordinary too, but fantastic rather than tiresome, mysterious not senile. I had never had a regular correspondent who lived so far away, nor one who seemed to find writing to me an occupation of such absorbing interest.

But the flow of living intervened. Perhaps Old Aunt Isabella grew tired of bombarding a great-niece who showed so little understanding of her many problems; perhaps I found things to do of a more compelling fascination. It would be hard now to say who first stopped writing to whom. One day the correspondence simply ceased to exist. Some time later a delicate old-fashioned brooch, with quivering mauve drops of amethysts, came down to me, to go in turn to my own great-niece.

Old Aunt Mary lived till her ninetieth year, in which her great-niece at last found the husband so often wished for. When she died, Kersland Street was abandoned and Old Aunt Eliza went to join Old Aunt Lucia. By that time I had grown up and gone away and it was a tiny great-great-niece who was taken to visit them, still too small to be fascinated by the 3D stereoscopic viewer.

The world of the Old Aunts was very remote from our own. They made efforts to bridge the gap; on our part there was no reciprocal endeavour. They had no influence on the present, no part in the future, and it was only occasionally that we caught a glimpse of the link they forged with our common past.

Not so the young aunts, whose presence even when absent permeated much of our lives.

4

Aunt Lillias

Inside or out we seldom saw Aunt Lillias without a hat. She was small and hunched, with a face that must in her youth have been softly sweet. She had the same rather limp hair which I myself inherited, and which, on the few occasions when her headgear was absent, she wore with a centre parting in wings wound round a fillet. One thin elegant hand constantly rose and fell to brush back a straying tendril.

Aunt Lillias had spent much of her adolescence combating tuberculosis, at home in the great cold house and in a sanatorium in Aberdeenshire. In the struggle she had lost the function of one lung, and death, which had taken a brother from an infectious disease when she was eight and another when she was fifteen from her own complaint, must often have seemed very near. She fought it off however to live a long and—within her own terms— vigorous life.

The obstinacy that is part of the equipment to survive of the invalid remained with her. In her gentle unyielding way Aunt Lillias could cause her sisters considerable irritation. When it became necessary to move from Crown Circus, Aunt Lillias was indefatigable in her search for a new home; she was also ruthless in her perfectionism, discarding one possibility after another. The decision to settle in Bute Gardens was made without her approval, and through the years she never let this be forgotten. Above all she held against the house the fact that she could not see Ben Lomond from the windows.

In due course Aunt Edith died and the honourable title of Miss Sloan descended on Aunt Lillias. Though she herself by now was in poor health and no longer capable of the more arduous duties concerned with running the household, Aunt Lillias refused to delegate any of the authority vested in her, unwilling to share the overseeing of the communal finances or to accept that certain keys might well be entrusted to younger members of the family. It says much for the patience and understanding of those sisters that, in spite of forgetfulness and muddle, they allowed her to retain her pre-eminence until the day she died.

Like Old Aunt Lucia, Aunt Lillias had an obsession with clothes. Not that they were necessarily new. To her sisters her appearances in lovat green or mist blue tweeds, a different check coat or a long forgotten dress, were a constant source of surprise and sometimes annoyance—not for public remark but a matter of comment behind a shielding hand. Like a squirrel with its hoard, Aunt Lillias collected clothes from a variety of sources, secreting them away, enjoying the uncertainties of choice, the bringing out for use of some long hidden costume.

'Two years since she last wore that one,' Aunt Evelyn would whisper making a comic face at my mother—but it might just as well have been twelve years, or even twenty. It was a family joke, edged with indignation, that Aunt Lillias, who suffered from migraine, never failed to rise from her bed and hasten into town on the days that the Spring and Autumn Sales started.

Her wardrobe was of such dimensions that her own bedroom could not contain it. All over the house, wherever there was a spare corner, Aunt Lillias's clothes infiltrated. When the young niece who lived with them returned to school the door was barely closed behind her before Aunt Lillias was making good use of the cupboard in her room.

But Aunt Lillias's appearance, unlike Old Aunt Lucia's, did not present an exotic jumble. Within her own range Aunt Lillias had a sense of colour and style. She enjoyed the possession of the clothes in her cupboards as much as wearing them and had no need for ostentatious display. Round her neck a small fur tippet in winter, a chiffon scarf in summer, was the only concession to what in the older aunts would have been the comfort of a woolly shawl. Occasionally, for no particular reason that I could discern, perhaps because a search or a tidy had revealed unsuspected treasures which, however, she could plainly no longer wear, Aunt Lillias made me a gift. Jade green pure silk with a black fringe that had once been part of a gown, an embroidered oriental shawl, a black chiffon velvet cloak lined with cerise. Almost certainly she told me where they came from: if so I have long forgotten. Perhaps some were relics of Old Aunt Tina or Old Aunt Jenty's time in India, or perhaps Old Aunt Mary once went to a ball in jade green silk; maybe Old Aunt Lucia herself had passed on some of her more choice pieces to this niece who also loved clothes.

People were Aunt Lillias's other consuming interest—particularly those with a family connection. She had made herself the recorder of the clan, and knew in the minutest detail who had married whom, when so-and-so had died, and what the relationship was between Cousin Charlie and the couple who lived in that place halfway to Gairloch. Debarred in her youth from the active life that her brothers and sisters enjoyed, Aunt Lillias had made herself the authority on the family history to whom they all deferred.

Her knowledge was not of the past only. Each day she read the

Glasgow Herald from cover to cover, and she had an eagle eye for items of news, however remote, which might come within the orbit of her special interest. She had a prodigious and infallible memory for the most minute grains of information. She was a prolific letter writer with a network of correspondents through whom she kept the clan in touch with all important events. One of her domestic jobs was to wash the net curtains at the windows and she was often to be seen holding them aside the better to see what was going on in the street.

Aunt Lillias loved to talk, and nothing gave her greater pleasure than to explore, without malice, the vagaries and complexities of human nature both in her own family and other people's. When recollection failed, or arguments with relatives threatened to become heated, my mother would say, 'Let's ask Lillias, she'll know what year we went there—or who we met—or how many children so-and-so had at the time', and if Aunt Lillias was not immediately at hand then my mother would not hesitate to resort to the telephone. When Aunt Lillias died, great tracts of the communal memory perished with her, and till the end of her own long life my mother frequently said when musing on the past, 'How I miss her. Aunt Lillias would have known that.'

The Royal Family ran the Sloans and their ramifications a close second in the competition for Aunt Lillias's attention. Queen Victoria's Diamond Jubilee had been celebrated when she was eighteen. Nine years before that the Queen herself had come to Glasgow to visit the Great Exhibition. Aunt Lillias knew all her descendants almost as well as she knew her own relations, and she scrutinised—though she rarely judged—their doings with the utmost attention. Not to be interested in the Sovereign and those near to him or her was a form of lèse majesté for which one sister-in-law was sharply reproved. 'But then I didn't know them as well as she did. She knew them *all*,' this aunt said somewhat apologetically, momentarily cowed by the implications of disloyalty.

The attachment to royalty had a more psychic side to it. My Grandmother had been warned of impending disasters by royal dreams, and my mother too, at one tragic moment of her life, swore that it had been preceded by a dream in which she met and talked with the King and Queen. As she only mentioned this some time after the event I was never quite certain in my own mind of the validity of this particular premonition. However, though I had noticed that the younger aunts scoffed when such forewarnings were mentioned, there had also seemed to me somewhat too much of protest in their repudiation. So for some years I kept a careful watch on my own dreams of royalty, invoking Grandmother Agnes as I did so—for after all, as I was not a seventh child nor had the second sight, it would have been a matter of personal prestige to have been singled out by the fates in this way. But alas I could discover no correlation between the many crises and trials of my adolescence and the infrequent glimpses of royal personages floating down the corridors of my dreams.

Her delicacy did not prevent Aunt Lillias from giving practical expression to her Christianity both at home, through the YWCA, the Bible Society and a multiplicity of other organisations, and overseas by the instrument of the Zenana Bible and Medical Mission, which her own aunts had been serving in India in the year in which she was born. She was a formidable attender of meetings and a good speaker at them. Stubbornly resisting bad weather and a short supply of breath, she would toil up the stone stairs of tenement after tenement, to collect subscriptions for the mission or the church, or venture out to spend long hours both in committee and exercising her great gift for conversation on behalf of and with her girls of the Young Women's Christian Association. Close after the Sloans and the Royal Family, their joys and sorrows were a matter of affectionate concern to her.

All the sisters enjoyed travelling, though their outward reactions often belied their adaptability when faced with new forms of transport and their pleasure in discovering fresh landscapes. My mother could never settle down to a journey until arrangements had been made for our escape if the worst happened and the train crashed. However, once she had decided to her own satisfaction that the lavatory window could be broken and we all knew where the communication cord was, she was then prepared to enjoy herself until the moment of impact. Faced late in life with incarceration in her first aeroplane she was very exercised by this question of possible escape, preferring always to have her own private arrangements quietly made rather than trust to the public ones.

Both Aunt Chrissie and Aunt Evelyn, being of excitable temperaments, accompanied any journey with exclamations of alarm or indignation whenever the performance of their own, or other people's, vehicles seemed in the slightest degree to warrant such expressions—and sometimes when it did not. But this vocal anguish was their natural accompaniment to nomadic enjoyment, and they had no conception of the genuine terror which their mother had felt on those unfortunate birthday outings.

Aunt Lillias shared this zest for peregrination, though she too had her own form of insurance against too much unadulterated felicity. What she should wear and what might be needed for comfort or in case of emergencies were all matters of concern. Until decisions were made on the necessity or otherwise of scarves, rugs, thermos flasks, books, bags, sweets and cushions, travel was to be endured rather than enjoyed.

In the nineteen-twenties and thirties it was Aunt Lillias who was sent out, like the dove from the ark, to find and inspect houses where they might come to rest for summer or Easter holidays. It could be that the choice fell on her because she was known to have strong views on such matters and an inclination to distrust the judgment of her sisters.

Armed with addresses, contacts, and the opinions of every other member of the family, Aunt Lillias made long railway journeys to the Highlands in early summer—going from Glasgow to Grantown-on-Spey in 1927, a distance of about one hundred and fifty miles, and back again, in two consecutive days. No aspect of her inspection on arrival would have been abandoned through fatigue or ill-health. On the contrary, it was certain that her enquiries had been penetrating and thorough. She would have looked at bedrooms, bathroom and probably the kitchen as well, discovered the distance to the golf course, where to order milk and how often the trains ran. Her report on returning home, in addition to practical information on prices, menus, hot water and walks, almost certainly included a run-down on the chosen landlady's family, as well as gleanings about who else was likely to holiday in Grantown that year, where they would stay and in what relation they stood to known friends. The prodigious energy required to undergo such marathons seemed always accessible to Aunt Lillias and to belie both her frail appearance and the fact, which was often mentioned to us, that she had only one lung.

In common with the rest of the aunts, she had an unquenchable appetite for picnics. On holiday, or staying with us in the country, one of her major pleasures was to eat a meal out of doors, preferably in landscape as wild, remote and beautiful as it was possible to reach by whatever transport was available. Weather hardly seemed to matter where these expeditions were concerned. Aunt Lillias took an optimistic view of even the greyest sky and was convinced that the notorious silver lining was always on the point of materialising behind every cloud.

What did matter, however, were certain material requisites for the ideal picnic place. It must have running water, for there was a kettle to be boiled, with a twig stuck in the spout to keep out the smoke—which it never did. Though my father carried an extremely temperamental portable stove, which endowed most picnics with a quota of singed eyebrows and reasons for vocal alarm, nevertheless it was important to make a fire and the ingredients for this had to be present within reasonable distance. Wandering the moors in a new/old tweed suit, her hair escaping in unruly strands from beneath the inevitable hat, Aunt Lillias had an eagle eye for what would burn and what would not. Fires sometimes caused friction, my mother also being persuaded that she alone knew how to set, coax and keep alight a good blaze.

Food too was not without its complications. Aunt Lillias was fussy, and she had good reason to treat her stomach with delicate respect. On the moors with the curlews calling and the peewits crying down the wind, while black-faced sheep champed boldly nearer and nearer wondering if they too could join in, invalid and other diets seemed more easily to meet and merge than they did at Bute Gardens. There, I gradually came to realise, the problems of accommodating one light meal in a menu otherwise healthily substantial were what lay behind the excesses of frog spawn sago and the subversive faces of Aunt Chrissie or Aunt Gertrude.

A flat spot for the food to be laid out on was important and a reasonable site to lay down rugs, or get out of the wind, or have protection if it rained—though in the latter case there were plenty of precedents for wet picnics huddled under bridges or conduct-ed with some difficulty inside the car. All things considered it was surprising how often the optimum conditions for a really good picnic were found—even taking into account my father's propen-sity for feeling that round the next corner we would always discover a better site and the fact that Sloan women always knew best.

A camera was part of the required baggage, so that a record could be taken before we actually packed up and left. Aunt Edith sitting bolt upright on a convenient stone, Aunt Lillias reclining near the fire, with essential items arranged round her, the younger aunts, skirts kilted and a stout stick in one hand, engaged in more daring activities, the whole surrounded by various nieces and nephews—this tableau appeared again and again in assorted photograph albums. What remained unre-corded was the gaiety, the laughter, the numerous small crises and adventures which Aunt Lillias would relate on future picnics—adding date, temperature, weather and exact map location—as on the current one she had regaled the party with tales of past outdoor meals stretching back over thirty, forty, eventually fifty and more years.

Not that she was content merely to be a recorder. She too added her quota to the accumulation of incident that wove into our background the inescapable pattern of family history. If there was a cottage nearby Aunt Lillias would find some pretext to accost the occupiers and talk with them: if a man with a horse and cart, a shepherd with his dog, a boy or girl going for a message, passed the picnic spot Aunt Lillias was loath to let them go without a word. Her interest was all-embracing, her readiness to respond unfailing. At least one small nephew found himself, then and later, warming to her passionate concern with the everyday joys and sorrows of humanity.

5

The Past

My mother was a Bronze Eagle. So too was Aunt Edith, but I am not sure that we relished having to share this honour. It was one we greatly admired, perhaps because it was one of the few Sloan sporting achievements that my brothers did not feel capable of surpassing. For my part sporting excellence was outside my range, but I was loyal to my relations in any rivalry between the generations.

The Bronze Eagle had been given for skating, a winter pastime that seemed to have occupied a good deal of the young Sloans' thinking between November and March.

Perhaps the power of this memory lay partly in the fact that we had visual evidence of its truth, quite apart from the Bronze Eagle itself, produced for inspection only on special occasions. Each winter one or two spells of clear cold weather would arrive, when a low sun slanted through the trees causing frosty twigs to sparkle and old puddles to turn to black steel mirrors. Then we piled on to bicycles or into the car and went to see if the Dyke pond was bearing. Skates came out to be greased and polished; chilblains, on feet squeezed into boots which felt a size too small, were almost forgotten. The delicate tests of balance, which had been mastered last year, were tried out again. Breath condensed in the air and our mother came into her own.

There was no doubt that she could skate. Her outside edges were more graceful and incisive than our shaky efforts. She could cut a figure of eight which we found great difficulty in emulating. Given a partner she could sweep across the ice in an elegant dance. Had we had the judging of it we would have given her a Bronze Eagle ourselves. Indeed we could not understand why it had not been a silver one.

In Glasgow skating took place on Bingham's Pond out the Great Western Road—Mr Bingham being the factotum who looked after pond affairs—and the Sloans were by no means the only Glasgow family that watched the thermometer as it fell and longed to escape from the classroom on to the ice. Skating half holidays were sometimes given, and on days without such a dispensation my mother, though not I suspect Aunt Edith, had been known to get into trouble for sitting in class with her boots on, ready to rush straight off to the pond as soon as the bell went. There seemed never to have been a winter without its spells of hard frost. In 1925 Grandfather, then eighty-two, was commenting on a visit he had made to the pond—'I do not remember ever having such severe and fairly long frost so *early*. The skating pond was bearing for a whole week but alas! the skaters were few as compared with long ago. . . Bingham was in great spirits and glad to see so many of the old faces again.'

It was Grandfather who taught his flock to skate, sweeping across the frozen water with folded arms, followed by a train of sons and daughters in ever-decreasing size. He was a committed curler too, sliding along the ice in plus-fours mopping furiously in front of the stone, and uttering from under his white moustache the inarticulate cries beloved of men who follow this sport.

Indoor rinks were unknown, and would not have been appreciated. The rural nature of Western Glasgow still permitted a number of small ponds, and bowling greens were flooded. In 1892 there had even been illicit skating on an unflooded bowling green in a sudden sharp snap. Much of the excitement lay in the unpredictability of the weather—lying awake at night testing the degree of frost with a twitching nose tip, gauging in the morning the intensity of the patterns iced on the window pane. Rumour and counter-rumour flew about, compounding the anguish of school hours when, for all one knew, time might be hastening on towards a thaw. Released into the tingling air, skates carried dangling from a strap clashing together with a sharp ringing clink, the sky white behind dark etched trees, or scarlet as the sun went down, the blood raced and the feet, so soon to float no longer earthbound, pounded on the crackling pavements.

Everybody in the district converged on the pond, among them the Sloans who were a noted skating tribe. They knew it, and enjoyed their brief moments of supremacy. For once the long skirts were no real handicap as Aunt Edith and her sisters glided hand in hand round the periphery of the ice, or individually, well aware that they were watched—and perhaps envied—curved and circled in the centre of an admiring audience. The youngest brother, on the tail of a whirling line in a dangerous exercise known as 'Port the Helm', knocked over his future wife one winter's day, and did not stay to answer her indignant query as to who that nasty little boy had been.

When, almost without warning, the surface of the ice dulled and dampened, the cutting whirr of the skates lost its sharpness and the lines of trees began to blur against a grey sky there was always some achievement left undone, a particular figure unattained, unless or until the smell of frost returned to the air and the electric anticipation began again.

The four oldest girls, Aunt Edith, Aunt Nancy, Aunt Lillias and my mother, went to a school conducted by a Miss Zimmerman, who was very small. This establishment occupied two houses in a nearby terrace, one of them as a boarding house, and it had a visiting male pedagogue who taught writing. My mother in later life regretted her lack of education, though the gaps she perceived may have been due more to her own involvement in activities out of school hours than Miss Zimmerman's shortcomings. Education for the girls was taken seriously by both Thomas Lucas Paterson and my Grandfather, and it was from the school in Westbourne Terrace that Aunt Nancy went on to become one of the earliest women medical graduates in Glasgow.

It never occurred to us that Aunt Edith or Aunt Lillias—or for that matter our mother—suffered from educational shortcomings. None of the things that my mother claimed not to have learnt seemed to have made any difference to their ability to conduct their own lives in a satisfactory manner, and the stock of dramatic and romantic poetry which they appeared able to recite at will, stirring our blood with the raising of the clans, message fires on Ben Ledi and the last days of old soldiers, was an enviable resource which our own schools failed to instil.

The three younger aunts had the advantage of a new modern girls' private school opened in 1903, from which Aunt Evelyn went on to Glasgow University. She never spoke of this experience, and within the family it was impossible to tell that there had been any variation in the formal education of the aunts. Perhaps their schooldays played little part in talk of the past because family activities were so much more interesting and exciting than anything that happened in the classroom, and the things they learned from their father, and each other, and the horde of relatives, more immediate and important.

Of those concerns their Christian faith and a love of outdoor pursuits had a high priority. If Grandfather skated with his tail of offspring behind him, he also bicycled accompanied by as many of his children as were free, or of an age, to do so. These cycle expeditions did not take the form of a sedate circling of the nearby Botanic Gardens; the intention was to get out of the spreading city into the glorious country beyond it, and if possible into the mountains. Sometimes the cycles would be loaded on to a train, with the ride as the return journey. Sixty miles was a reasonable run, unless memory had exaggerated somewhat—a distance that to us, already seduced by the motor car, seemed prodigious. Speculating on their encumbering apparel and the primitive nature of the bicycles, as compared to our own, we could not imagine how the aunts had done it. But I did not doubt that they had. There was too much circumstantial detail.

A favourite incident was that of Grandfather free-wheeling down a steep hill, with two or three sons and daughters behind him. Suddenly, coming to a corner, he was no longer visible. There was a wagonette climbing in the opposite direction and Grandfather, who had been momentarily disconcerted by the suddenness of this apparition, was discovered in a somewhat undignified position in the ditch having taken a full toss over the handlebars. Picked up by his daughters and dusted down, he set off again as if nothing had happened.

The bicycles went on holiday too, those holidays which were the highlights of the year, when attachments to certain parts of the country were formed of such strength that any projected change encountered fierce resistance. Every mountain road or loch shore had its memories, each village bothy its story. Every local character was known, their family-history lovingly recon-structed in the winter evenings. Strathyre for instance, where a limerick made up by a favourite cousin about my mother survived to be repeated to her daughter—though as a warning or a comfort I was never sure.

'There was a young maid of Strathyre,
Who daily grew higher and higher,
Till walking one night
She found to her fright
She could touch the telegraph wire.'

It was at Strathyre that Grandfather, coming up from Glasgow on Fridays to join his wife and children, threw the week-end joint out ot the train window to waiting catchers, as it steamed slowly into the station past the garden of their holiday house. And it was from Strathyre that Granny, Aunt Nancy and the cook, for one week in September, returned to Crown Circus to make jam leaving Aunt Edith to look after the family.

There were stories too of struggling up Ben Vorlich—or was it Ben Ledi of watchfire fame—to see the sunrise, maddened by the greater physical ease which trousers afforded to the brothers and so abandoning heavy dew-sodden skirts in favour of the freedom of elasticated knickers.

Or we would go to Crianlarich, at the junction of the railways to Oban and Mallaig, where the endless romance of trains and engines could be enjoyed; amd Dalmally, at the foot of Ben Cruachan and the Pass of Brander, with its memories of fishing trips on Loch Awe and Aunt Edith presiding over picnics while the catch was assessed. There the first Gaelic words were learned, which we ourselves tried out a generation later on a bewildered young man called Charlie in a grocer's shop on Mull. The Sloan sisters' Gaelic may not have been very adequate, but the dramatic emphasis with which they rolled out the phrases more than made up for inaccuracies. Perhaps some of the fascination with things Highland, and the language, had originated in the open-air Sunday evening meetings of Glasgow's Gaelic speakers, mainly female domestics and off-duty policemen which took place in the late 1800s at the junction of the Byres Road and Great Western Road, not far from Crown Circus.

Later the holidays moved further north still, to Grantown and Nethy Bridge in the Cairngorms where there were good golf courses, or Deeside where Aunt Lillias had spent so much of her youth in a sanatorium at Banchory and now could indulge her passion for the Royal Family to the full at Ballater and Balmoral.

By comparison with those vividly remembered days, the

incidents, the personalities, the long walks over the heather, the fish cooked fresh on a wood fire, the escapades, above all the sense of crowded enjoyment of a multi-faceted family life at full pressure, our own summer holidays seemed unadventurous and even rather tame. I saw the Highlands of Scotland at second-hand, through the eyes of my mother and her sisters, reinforced by the stirring tales of Scottish history. Indeed the two were not always distinguishable. Driving through Dalmally we would watch out for the spot on the road where a pony trap had overturned, or the very stone—was it, was it not?—on which an attempt had been made to fry eggs in the sun. Driving through Glencoe we heard of the betrayal of the Macdonalds by the Campbells—to whom too we happened to be related.

Those were the summer holidays, when Grandfather and the older boys came to join the family group as business permitted, but a fortnight at Easter was also spent out of the city. In this instance we had an even closer connection with those far-off times, for many of the shorter holidays had been taken in Dumfriesshire, in the big farmhouse at Beattock two and a half miles down the road from Moffat, where we ourselves lived.

Beattock was tiny, straggling along the Glasgow-Carlisle road with the main north-south railway line behind it. The square old farmhouse stood at the end of the village facing the turn-off that ran into the hills of Moffat at the foot of the Beef Tub. It was a stylish grey stone house with white bordered windows and a portico. The outward appearance, and that of the farmyard behind it, had changed very little since the aunts explored the cart sheds, made friends with the sheepdogs, terrified each other with stories about the bull, and had a group photograph taken in the field in front. The house had been an old one in their day—as it was in ours.

Moffat was a spa. It had waters smelling of rotten eggs drawn from a well about two miles beyond the town—or, for those who could not manage this steep walk, dispensed at certain times in the Baths Hall in the High Street. In our youth too the well water was still drunk as a cure and our father used to take us up for a glass—as our grandfather had taken his family—joking as he did so that it was the walk and not the water that had a beneficial effect. Smelling that repulsive, somehow thick, beverage, we had no difficulty in imagining the reactions of the younger aunts.

In their day, coaches had come over the Beef Tub from Edinburgh, to set down and take up at the Buccleuch Arms Hotel in the High Street. There had been boat trips on the park pond, and even on one occasion the great excitement of a dancing bear.

But the real memories were of the children's activities—some of them, we could not help feeling, undertaken in Grandfather's absence and without the knowledge of Granny! Rides on the farmer's cart behind the great snorting horses, watching the dogs herd the sheep, visits to Beattock station to see the London trains pull in, while they waited for the extra engine to be attached at the rear for the long haul up the summit. It was occasionally possible, if the summit engine driver was a known friend and in a good mood, to get taken on a joy-ride, puffing asthmatically up the steep gradient behind the heavy train until the summit was reached at Elvanfoot, only to come spinning back down to Beattock free both of weight and duty.

The most daring undertaking on the railway line, and one which my mother sometimes regretted retelling to my brothers, was the use of it as a mint to double the meagre store of pocket money. Sneaking around the back of the station to a spot some hundred yards north and sheltered by sheds, they would place halfpennies on the line before a train was due to pass and then retire to a hiding place to watch. Given a skilful placement and some luck the result could be an emaciated blurred coin which might be passed off as a penny at the village shop. The aunts would deny that they had ever taken part in this attempted deceit, blaming the boys, but there was a look of awakened memory in their eyes that seemed to indicate a rather closer involvement than simply hearsay.

Of all the sights and scenes we shared with our aunts' youth
the Beattock village shop was the most immediate. A minute, all-
purpose store created out of the front room of a cottage in the
middle of a row it was presided over by Maggie Hutchieson. In
our day she was very old, with the hairy nutcracker appearance
that befitted one who was a denizen from the past. For Maggie
Hutchieson, and a sister long since dead, had presided over the
Beattock shop when the aunts were in the farmhouse for Easter
holidays, and had been on the look-out then—as Maggie was
now—for squashed halfpennies passing themselves off as pen-
nies.

She was a small woman, to us an ancient immortal, with bright
blue eyes and a loud cracked voice, still perfectly capable of
chasing the boys out of the shop if they attempted any sleight of
hand with her sweeties. She called my mother 'Miss Mora', and
enjoyed reminiscing about the Sloan family. We half believed she
was a witch and were frightened of, and fascinated by, her. Her
obvious conviction that it was we, as the offspring of one of those
far-off children, who were the oddities was disconcerting, and her
uninhibited comments about us shrivelled us up. Yet we greatly
enjoyed visiting her, dimly recognising that she connected us in
some way more vividly with the past than even the aunts
themselves. Besides, the shop with its jars of coloured sweets
and its bins of essential staples had a savour all its own. We
always came away with a pennyworth of tiny pink and white
rosebuds, because that had been a favourite purchase of my
mother and her sisters all those years before.

Worship played a consistent part in family life, whether at
home or on holiday. Prayers were after breakfast, with everyone
from the latest baby to the newest little maid taking part.
Thanksgiving came before a meal, which presupposed punctual
arrival and a certain seemliness of demeanour. On Sundays they
walked to service, across the park, over the heather, down the
village street or, in the case of Beattock, along the road and up
the field path to the isolated little church with its square box

pews—inside which it was sometimes possible to play unlawful games unseen—and the long-handled wooden ladles which were poked over the pew doors for collection.

Grandfather's church-going was a pleasure rather than a duty and the children were not oppressed by it, being quite capable of imitating the drawn-out, lilting accent of a Highland minister and enjoying the human frailties of the congregation. They respected the elders of the kirk, but were not intimidated by them. Having been taught to study the Word for themselves, and being accustomed to the reading of it as an everyday theme, each one in his or her own way recognised the need for an independent relationship with God and a personal faith.

In such a large family there was little room for indulgence. Discipline was essential; there were always younger children to be looked after, clothes were handed down—to the considerable annoyance of those who came at the end of the line—pocket money was modest. But there was no attempt to dragoon the children into a preconceived pattern. As they grew up the girls proved to have very different characters and these were allowed to flower in their own ways. Granny may have been preoccupied with babies for the first twenty years of her marriage, but she did not find her children a burden on her spirit. Grandfather, from the time of the birth of his oldest son, took an active pleasure in his growing family. No single one of them ever felt unwanted or undervalued, and in the flood of memories that played so large a part in their relationship with us punishment was never mentioned. Not that it was unknown. There must have been many moments when both sternness and retribution became inevitable. But they left few marks because the strength of unquestioned family affection, and the certainty of discovering at least one sympathiser among so many, sustained the culprit and eased whatever pain had been caused.

Of course there were disadvantages in so large and close-knit a group. Privacy was at a premium. Little could be concealed, either physically, or of thought, feeling or opinion. Criticism was uninhibited and combined scorn occasionally daunting. Perhaps this was why my mother, who had suffered from having a hoydenish preference for the pursuits of the two brothers immediately younger than herself, laid great stress on our never being critical. There were times when it required strength of character to sustain a conviction of personal worth; in turn this resulted later in the fortitude required to come to terms with the good and evil of life which was a marked characteristic of each of the aunts.

With a range of twenty years between the oldest and the youngest, however, the possibilities of changing alliances to meet whatever crises arose were endless. Family solidarity was strong and instantly alerted at any threat from the outside world to one member or to the group as a whole. In the last analysis love was what counted.

6

Aunt Chrissie

Aunt Chrissie was an artist. She offered an alternative to my missionary aspirations, and one for which I had somewhat more aptitude. Gradually the service of the evangelist was discarded for the self-indulgence of the artist. Unable to translate into words feelings of even quite trivial a nature I viewed with relief the possibility of expressing inner convictions through a different medium. Aunt Chrissie herself was articulate, as well as being an able draughtswoman, but in my teens this quality seemed to be beyond my reach. Contrary however to my feelings when I thought of emulating Old Aunt Jenty or Old Aunt Tina in the mission field I had no doubt that I would outshine Aunt Chrissie in the exercise of her other talent, and this belief—based on an underestimate of her skills and an over-confidence in my own— probably indicated the correctness of my choice of model.

Aunt Chrissie herself did her best to encourage me, taking me on visits to the Art Galleries, inviting me into the private haven of her bedroom to see the latest collection of holiday watercolours or a piece of beautifully illuminated calligraphy undertaken as a commission. I was both elated at being singled out and tongue-tied in the presence of her work. She can never have guessed at the unfounded and misplaced arrogance which whispered to me that some day I would do a great deal better. I had no idea that I would come to admire more justly the elegance and wit of her line and the purity of her colour—when it was too late to talk to her about them.

Christina Scott Paterson was the oldest of the group of three girls that finished off the Sloan family. From her earliest youth she had been what was known as a 'card', bursting with ideas and initiative, prepared to go out and forge pathways for herself, with a flair for the dramatic which made her conspicuous in both presence and appearance. She had the nervous, self-centred temperament which can go with those attributes and in her younger days she often did not take kindly to the robust competitive life of a big family. She was a crybaby, which in the sisters evoked teasing rather than sympathy. As usual, however, numbers made comfort possible. In a crisis she went for consolation to one of the big brothers. When the situation was reversed, as could happen very suddenly, Aunt Chrissie was not slow to take her turn as tormentor.

She undertook professional training at Glasgow School of Art, in Charles Rennie Mackintosh's new building. That she was able to do so in the early years of the century was a sign of the humanity and liberality of her parents' outlook, for her mother had strong views on the theatre, dancing and reading novels before four o'clock in the afternoon—all of which were to be eschewed—and art school, with its overtones of Bohemianism and nude models, might easily have joined this catalogue. Nor was there any family tradition of practical artistic work to weigh in the balance—except Old Aunt Lillias' china painting, and that hardly counted.

It was not, of course, envisaged that Aunt Chrissie would leave home and set up as a working artist. Such a step would indeed have taken her across certain well-defined, if invisible, boundaries. Perhaps the respectable custom of young ladies being encouraged to cultivate a gift for painting in watercolours was in Granny's mind when she agreed to her daughter taking this step. Or was it, more profoundly, that remembering the restrictions in her own life she wanted her girls to have as much freedom as possible to develop their individual talents?

For Aunt Chrissie, her art was a much more serious business than a pleasant amusement to occupy her until she married. It was not a diversion for spare moments, but a part of her very nature and indivisible from it, the expression of which shaped her view of life. Remembering the rebellious bitterness which flooded my heart on hearing my own efforts to become a painter spoken of as a 'nice hobby' I wonder now what furies of revolt may not sometimes have overturned Aunt Chrissie's soul when she was young.

It was not that the family lacked appreciation of her talent. In her seventies Granny submitted to having her portrait painted, a worn-out old woman with a strong bony face, a purple satin cape trimmed with fur round her shoulders. When Aunt Chrissie exhibited, the sisters went to see and admire, but this aspect of her life was subordinate to the pressures of a communal household, the duties and affections of family life and the pull of family pursuits. She never had a studio, and when I wanted to go to art school my mother said, 'I don't know where you get it from', which indicated an undervaluing of Aunt Chrissie's gift. No wonder that, every now and then, she asserted her individuality by taking a job or travelling to study in galleries and to exercise her own art. But, whatever frustrations she may herself have encountered, she was, and remained, unfailingly generous and encouraging towards other, younger artists.

About the time when the Great War began there was a spate of family marriages. My mother was on her honeymoon in Norway

in August 1914, separated from her home by what she feared was
a submarine infested sea. The year before her older sister, Aunt
Nancy, who had found a prospective husband in India, married
him in Glasgow, and Aunt Chrissie's comforter in the family,
Uncle Wilfrid, had settled down with a wife. While in 1915 Aunt
Evelyn was on the high seas en route to India, accompanying my
mother's new sister-in-law who was to marry another brother,
the little boy who had knocked her down on the skating pond.
Aunt Chrissie, in her late twenties, must have felt that matrimony
might be just around the corner for her too.

Instead she was caught up in the war—which was to stand in
our minds as the single compelling reason for her celibacy and
that of her sisters. Whether this judgment was true in actuality we
never knew. Psychologically it provided a vindication of their
unmarried state.

Aunt Chrissie went to France to serve with the Scottish
Churches Huts, accompanied by a girl friend. She took with her
sketchbooks and pencils, and her own observant wit. Under a
drawing of three male figures in outrageous striped bathing suits
paddling in the sea at Paris Plage she wrote a caption: 'Sea
Weeds: very common on the French Coast, always found in
shallow water.' A few pages farther on a riposte is stuck into the
album, a picture of Aunt Chrissie in a large flat hat sitting
sketching on a sand dune. Below it the artist, who signed himself
simply 'Robin' had written, 'Common objects of the seashore. No
1, The Glasgow Evening Argus.' She may not have had a hundred
eyes, but the two she did possess served her very well.

The Lewis Gun School occupied Le Touquet Golf Course.
Coming from a family who loved the game, playing it well herself,
did this use of the greens and fairways strike her as sacrilegious?
She worked at Etaples, helping in the military hospital, earning
the gratitude of the Red Cross, and later, in 1918, with No 8 Red
Cross Hospital, Boulogne, to which she found her own way from
London by the South East and Chatham Railway on a second
class ticket costing nineteen shillings and sevenpence. It was

hard to imagine her nursing, or dealing efficiently with daily administration. She had little head for the details of life and no sense of time—though in a remarkable way she always knew what the time was but never managed to use it punctually. In September 1919 she travelled officially to Bonn and Cologne on a Provost Marshal's pass, with a seat reserved in the Ladies Coach. No doubt she entertained her fellow ladies hilariously with her reconstruction of 'incidents', gesticulating with her elegant bony hands, her bright brown artist's eyes alert to gauge reactions and build on to them with additional dramatic emphasis.

There were stories too told through gales of laughter of other, less segregated, expeditions by staff car and the embarrassments of uncertain toilet facilities. The occasion when, having asked to wash her hands, Aunt Chrissie was confounded by the innkeeper's wife yelling to her husband for the key of the 'cabinet' for Mademoiselle. Then there was the time in the officer's mess when, unsure of the geography of the house, she and her friend opted for the overnight use of a tin wastepaper basket—only to find in the morning a potty discreetly hidden in a cupboard.

But war was not only amusing happenings, dancing Maori soldiers or military sports with special races for the VADs. In April 1917 the battle of Arras began fifty miles to the west of Etaples. The brother Wilfrid, who had been her defender in the days when she had been dubbed a crybaby, was shot through both legs and lay all day in a shell hole in agony. He was a man who loved life and nature, full of zest and optimism. After dark his comrades brought him in and he was taken to base hospital at Camières, close to Etaples, where one leg was amputated. Fourteen days later, with his wife at his side, he died of gangrene.

Aunt Chrissie got permission to go to Camières as soon as the news reached her. This time she had the most difficult of all roles to play, to sustain her sister-in-law and watch her brother die. Her temperament was one more naturally at home with the crises and adventures of an active life. Unlike her older sisters, patient comforting did not come easily to her and her usual response in the face of sickness and suffering was to recoil. But in this bitter moment she put aside every customary instinct, finding in herself a strength and a gentleness that were remembered with gratitude to the end of a long life by her sister-in-law. For Aunt Chrissie this experience was one of which we never heard her speak, however wide ranging the spate of family reminiscence.

Whether the universal catastrophe of the war brought her an even more intimate sorrow we never knew. She enjoyed joking about past boy friends, young men met in circumstances which she depicted as extraordinary, bizarre or horrendous—though often one suspected that much of the glamour surrounding such encounters was flung over them in retrospect, like a lacy sequined veil spun out of her vivid imagination. To the end of her life any personable man invoked in her a not always unconscious flirtatiousness and admiration. But behind this sparkling camouflage the genuine affections of her heart, which for reasons tragic or trivial had failed to blossom, were carefully concealed. When she died, a watch belonging to one of the young men who had been killed was found among her possessions.

In 1919 her eldest brother's wife died leaving four young children. In the aftermath of the bereavement it was decided that one of the unmarried sisters should take over his household. Uncle Norman set his heart on having Aunt Evelyn.

She however was otherwise engaged and needed time to make her own arrangements, so, much against her will, Aunt Chrissie was persuaded for a period to act as a substitute mother. It was not a success. Scatty and uncoordinated, invariably late, with no sense of domestic order or ability to plan ahead on behalf of others, unable under such circumstances to reserve for her own use the periods of time alone that her temperament and her art demanded, the strain on both Aunt Chrissie and a brother sixteen years older than herself proved too great. Nor did the offer of Old Aunt Eliza and Old Aunt Lucia to accompany the family on a summer holiday and look after the children turn out any better. If Uncle Norman had been convinced from the beginning that Aunt Evelyn was his best choice, his judgment was amply vindicated during this disastrous time.

Nevertheless when, many years later, death at last brought Aunt Chrissie to fill the prized position of Miss Sloan, she insisted, as her sisters had done, on the full duties and status of that situation being accorded to her—though Aunt Evelyn, by then returned to the family nest, was both willing and more able to make the daily plans and undertake the duties required.

In the late 1920s the young niece came home from India, to live at Crown Circus and go to school. Aunt Chrissie went out to Jhansi, to keep her brother company for the six months while his wife was in Scotland with their daughter. She did not confine herself to the family circle, eventually staying two years, taking a job in an orphanage in Kalimpong, visiting Kashmir, painting everywhere she went. She would describe a face seen in a market place, a tableau on a river bank where women and children gathered to wash their clothes, the bride at a village wedding barely glimpsed behind her veils of scarlet and gold and the profusion of her jewellery. With eloquent hands, half-shut eyes bringing the picture into sharp perspective in her mind, thin sensitive lips puckered, she would draw out the words that tried to communicate to us her intense visual pleasure. The jewel-like quality of Mogul miniatures, which she saw reflected in tiny vignettes of human activity caught in the brilliant clear light of northern India, delighted her. A vision of water, blossom trees and the high snow mountains threw her into ecstasies. Somewhere too in these travels there was an incident involving her heart which, uncharacteristically, she would neither embroider nor conceal, beginning the story with her usual flair only to stop, tantalisingly, half-way through, refusing to reveal what had actually happened.

All this was behind her when we first became conscious of Aunt Chrissie as the eccentric member of the coterie of aunts in Glasgow. We enjoyed her fluidity. Aunts were permitted to be eccentric in a way that parents were not. Though she had the ability to wound with words and could openly take sides against us in a way that the others did not, we never brooded over the injustice of such interventions. Aunt Chrissie was not expected to be predictable.

She was the highlight of visits, introducing an element of sparkling uncertainty, glimpses of different, more exotic worlds, and a sense of values which, while still based on the solid virtues of her family and ours, yet made room for art and adventure and the flowering of personal initiative. There was a daring, a flavour of heightened perceptions and unfamiliar excess about her that kept us admiring and aware.

In appearance she was of middle height, bony with a sallow skin. Her face, full of character, the French would have called 'jolie laide'. It had elements of an ikon in it being oblong with strongly marked features, dark eyes, and a thin mouth tucked between full lower cheeks. But the ikon's immobility was totally lacking. This face, with its brown hair parted in the middle, was constantly in motion. At a glance it was possible to see instantly Aunt Chrissie's reaction to any situation, from the state of the weather to a bad accident in the road outside—and if, in the latter case, her expression felt itself to be failing to achieve the maximum effect, the hands, with their long ringed fingers, would join in. Her laugh was high-pitched, rising to a shriek then dying away in a bubbling gurgle like the call of some forest bird.

Aunt Chrissie's clothes were orchestrated with care and the result was often oriental in its use of colour and pattern. She enjoyed wearing the flamboyant—yellows, reds and browns, with a dash of madder or crimson, lime or violet in a floating scarf or embroidered shoulder bag. Jewellery, chosen for effect not value, delighted her—bracelets, Indian or Victorian, jangling on her skinny wrists, semi-precious cairngorms or inherited cameos catching back a kerchief or a cape. Sitting amid the coloured glass of Cranston's Tea Rooms, in a tight cloche hat, licking the cream from cakes off her fingers and giggling at a schoolboy nephew's jokes, Aunt Chrissie could appear more Art Nouveau than her setting.

This conspicuous bird of paradise nevertheless had her permanent home in the common nest. To us there were no obvious frictions. The strong core of loyalty and affection held—though Aunt Chrissie must often have longed for space, a studio and the independence to arrange her life as she pleased. The others must have had times when her inadequate time-keeping and inability to maintain a regular framework was a sore trial. But the shared concern was greater than anything that divided them. Aunt Chrissie too skated, golfed, walked and cycled, admired their father and indulged in the delicious pastime of unravelling the family grapevine.

She was also the instigator of many special activities, as she was the originator of numerous—and often alarmist—rumours. It was Aunt Chrissie who initiated the annual 'Sausage Sizzle' on Loch Ard in late September when, surrounded by nieces and nephews, brothers and sisters, she helped to fry sausages over a wood fire as the sun went down, eating them in the gloaming in a ceremony of farewell to the summer. It was Aunt Chrissie who acted in the plays at the great Christmas gatherings, reducing the cast round her to such a state of hysterical uncertainty that it was a matter of astonishment to everyone involved, audience and actors alike, when a coherent entity actually materialised. It was Aunt Chrissie who ensured that for several months we hardly dared to eat a banana, because of some connection between that fruit and intestinal worms which she claimed to have discovered—or even, horror of horrors, to have suffered from! It was Aunt Chrissie, always late, who was invariably left behind when the small procession of aunts and nieces left Crown Circus to walk across the park to church, and who was discovered, with some annoyance, to be sitting in the pew when they arrived having travelled by tram. And it was Aunt Chrissie who on one occasion incurred grave sisterly displeasure by leaving a niece alone in a cinema, to enjoy the film a second time round, at a moment when Glasgow was seized with panic at reports of trafficking in white slaves to South America.

Till she was in her old age she retained the ability to surprise. The friend with whom she had gone to war married a teacher, who eventually became headmaster of his own preparatory school in the south of England. In times of staffing difficulties Aunt Chrissie was often called upon to help out. She was a resourceful teacher, skilful at the construction of models and designing of projects, and in mathematics at looking up the answers before her pupils. In her seventies, during a period of crisis, she agreed to live in and look after the smallest boys, who enjoyed her lessons but for whom the real excitement was her appearance on the soccer field. She not only refereed, but also taught the rudiments of the game. It was not one she knew or understood, being more familiar with the rules of rugby football which one of her brothers had played for Scotland.

When questioned about how she managed to hold her own with two teams of screaming nine and ten-year-olds she giggled and replied: 'I've got the whistle—and besides they don't know any better than I do what should happen. I just make it up and tell them to get on with it.' In certain situations, it seemed, even handling of the ball was not totally forbidden.

Later still than this she went to pay a visit to a nephew and his family and, seeing bicycles lying around, clambered on to one, although she had not ridden for many years. With incoherent cries, thin legs driving like pistons, yellow scarf floating out behind, Aunt Chrissie pedalled round and round the garden, gaining momentum until she disappeared down a grassy slope. Screams rose from the invisible valley below. Transfixed by alarm the nephew held his breath. Her great-nephews rushed to have the first sight of disaster.

They abandoned her too soon. Puffing, triumphant, still on two wheels, she appeared again riding along the bottom of the ridge.

Invited, with Aunt Evelyn, to visit another nephew in the Bahamas, Aunt Chrissie outfitted herself for the occasion with the pleasure of a young girl. The house was close to a secluded beach, the water was clear, the sand white, the heat, which she had always enjoyed, delicious. Holding their skirts high the two aunts paddled, but my sister-in-law noticed that Aunt Chrissie's enthusiasm was muted and felt that her zest for life was failing her at last. It was only when the visit was over that she learnt the truth. Aunt Chrissie had invested in a new bathing suit and, not liking to usurp her hostess' prerogative by suggesting such a thing, was bitterly disappointed because swimming had never been on the programme.

Several years before, on holiday with her in Belgium where she shared a bedroom with my mother, I had occasionally surprised Aunt Chrissie in a state of undress, attempting with much dilly-dallying to decide which of her outfits she would wear that day. Her skin was like old parchment, her breasts flat withered pouches. That over ten years later she should have so little self-consciousness about her body and so much relish for physical enjoyment filled me with astonishment and admiration. For myself I had never bathed since, as a teenager, I had imagined the sight of my lanky, spindle-thin carcase to be as offensive to other people as, in imagination, it was to me.

Aunt Chrissie had self-confidence and elan, and a continuing and intense curiosity about the habits, customs and appearance of her fellow creatures, which embraced the world and gave her a readiness to make contact with any human being prepared to respond. She had a strong sense of Christian values and would not hesitate to take up the cudgels for any cause she considered just, whether it was a woman being unfairly treated on a bus or some more far-reaching wrong to be righted. But if she spoke of these things it was often within the dramatic, self-mocking framework of an 'incident' which we could all enjoy.

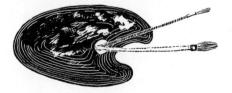

7

Gatherings

Music was not an art that our Grandmother felt to have close affinities with the devil though, probably arising from the bad reputation of actresses in her youth, she did dislike the theatre. This antipathy must at times have been difficult to reconcile with the obvious dramatic gifts of some of her brood. My mother used to say how much she would have liked to have gone on the stage. There had never been the remotest possibility of such a thing, but her voice held more regret for lack of talent and opportunity than the memory of parental anathema. Although in our youth a lingering flavour of forbidden fruit added spice to our rare visits to a live performance, the fact that this first happened at a comparatively late age was due more to country isolation than to vestiges of grandparental disapproval.

On the other hand the age of home entertainment flourished.

My father played the piano and sang; my mother recited with histrionic fervour. Our turn came at the Christmas parties.

For thirty years, first at Crown Circus with Grandfather, then at the home of our eldest uncle, and finally under the direction of a senior cousin, these gatherings acted as the focal point of the year for the larger family. They drew the threads together, revived the grapevine, introduced the extraneous elements added by marriage or by birth, and richly reinforced the stock of anecdote and incident. In the way of such assemblies they were both festive occasion and ferocious ordeal.

The parties took place after Christmas. Though in later years they became purely social, centred round a buffet lunch, in the days when my cousins and I were still the children they were altogether more formidable affairs, involving an overnight stay, a Christmas dinner and an individual performance. It was this latter item that caused us to look forward to them with mixed feelings.

For the aunts, both old and young, this was a moment when their place within the family was re-established, their importance underlined, and their function as a essential link in the communal life reinforced. The Old Aunts commanded by their stately presence the respect that they took for granted as their due. The irreverent speculation of some of her juniors as to Old Aunt Lucia's probable costume and adornment in no way detracted from the sense of awe which accompanied her actual appearance as she sailed into the drawing room loaded with beads and bracelets, shrouded in satin's and jet, her wall eye glaring terrifyingly at whichever young relative happened to be within its sightless orbit. On one of the few occasions on which she was present Old Aunt Mary, trumpet poised, sat next to the only great-niece whose voice she could distinguish. Both were incapable of eating, the one from age, the other from excitement.

For the young aunts it was a time of licence, when talents and personalities had an audience prepared to admire, applaud, criticise (in an undertone and with affection), but never condemn. They too had their sartorial glories, each in her own way producing the ultimate in her wardrobe—Aunt Edith in red satin set off by an embroidered shawl, Aunt Lillias in sea-blue silk hoarded away many moons before, her hat discarded in favour of a bandeau. Aunt Chrissie, jostling to hold the centre of the stage, dazzling the eye with colour combinations of unimagined brilliance, invariably swept into the room late. Once, clad in a maroon and gold tunic, she had difficulty during the meal keeping her napkin on her knees. When she rose from the table it was to discover that she had failed to put on her skirt and was wearing only a taffeta petticoat—fortunately also maroon.

The earliest parties, staged upstairs in the large light drawing room at Crown Circus, after dinner round the great table in the gloomy dining room below, held formidable terrors for me—and for all I knew for brothers and cousins too—at least until my own part in them was finished. I had no social talents and, even among relations, was painfully shy. But those drawbacks and afflictions were no excuse for not making a contribution. For days beforehand I had been dreading the moment when I should have to expose myself to the scrutiny of an audience made cheerfully iconoclastic by food, company and the festive spirit. No matter that the gaze would be kindly as well as quizzical. I knew very well that whatever I did would be made worse by nervous agitation and the sense that I was failing to uphold my section of the family in the face of more talented and composed cousins.

When Aunt Lillias sat down at the piano and Aunt Edith in full voice was heard advancing down the stairs, at the top of which she had been adding a final touch of drama to her toilet, I was unable to join in the subdued hilarity that trembled through the nieces and nephews—and even some of the older generation. When she pranced into the room singing 'Coming through the Rye' or 'The bonnie, bonnie banks o' Loch Lomond' I could not join in the applause, so preoccupied was I with the inexorable movement of time towards my own turn.

In the early years it took the form of a sword dance. No matter that the sword dance was really for little boys, it was the only form of solo entertainment of which I was capable, requiring no vocal effort and enabling me to keep my eyes fixed on the slats of wood which formed the swords.

Through the initiative of parents there was a dancing class one afternoon a week in our village. The teacher, highly recommended, came from Glasgow to put us through our paces in the Masonic Hall. She was a large woman with a magnificent bust down which dripped heavy strings of coloured beads and a way of counting in an emphatic voice which was all too easily imitable: 'One—two—three—FAH!'

One glorious afternoon her necklace broke, spattering the wooden floor with bijouterie which disappeared in all directions, down cracks, under chairs, behind the handbags of mothers and nannies. They were followed by every boy in the room, pushing and shoving, squeaking and laughing, anxious only to prolong this freedom from regimentation by adding to the general confusion, driving poor Miss Hazeldene, who clearly valued both the beads and her professional reputation, into a frenzy of agitation.

It cannot have been an easy assignment. Most of the boys considered dancing an activity wholly beneath them, enjoying only the more riotous polkas and gallops and reluctant to be seen putting their arms round little girls. For myself, longing only to be inconspicuous, those were hours of torment. The most enjoyable portion of the afternoon was that devoted to highland dancing. The exhilaration of the reels, just this side of being wild, the call of something altogether more primitive than foxtrot or waltz, released us all from the tensions and traumas of more genteel proceedings.

Admittedly the drawing room at Crown Circus, with all eyes focused on me, and Grandfather's gramophone subtly differing in the music it produced from the one that Miss Hazeldene so ably manipulated, seemed to do something uncontrollable to my feet. But at least when the exhibition was finished I could retire into the background and begin to enjoy the party.

Later on, heroic poetry became a feature of our contribution. My mother's predilection for declamation had accustomed us to it as a party piece. Even so my older brother, on one occasion, only agreed to perform if he was permitted to wrap himself in the window curtain. My own memory holds a different moment, of intense hero worship, when I saw him stand up, splendidly kilted and in full view, to recite with bloodcurdling emphasis:

'On Linden when the sun was low,
All bloodless lay the untrodden snow,
And dark as winter was the flow
Of Iser, rolling rapidly.'

A certain amount of discreet competition among those whose offspring were performing was inevitable. Sometimes there was a feeling that unfair advantage had been taken. One small cousin recited a poem in French, while her older brother played the piano—without music! Both those feats were held to indicate children of exceptional cleverness and there were one or two murmurs that this was not perhaps the spontaneous offering which the occasion required. But the aunts, delighted with every turn of whatever standard, and prepared moreover to expose themselves to us, in song, recital or drama, ensured an atmosphere of continuing hilarity. They joined in the games. There was a round game called 'The Princess is a lovely child', and a balloon game where the tall boy cousins always got possession. There were Hunt the Thimble, Postman's Knock, and Musical Bumps with Aunt Edith playing the piano, and of course there were charades.

When my two young brothers were about ten and twelve, greatly daring they composed a skit on a popular song, 'There's a hole in my bucket, dear 'Liza', but featuring Aunt Chrissie and Aunt Evelyn who were known to have been the central participants in a saga of seasickness on a holiday journey. Sung as a duet, accompanied on the piano by the youngest, this schoolboy humour was greeted with hysterical laughter and prolonged applause. No one enjoyed it more than Aunt Chrissie and Aunt Evelyn, unless it was one sister-in-law, sitting helpless, with tears rolling down her cheeks, while her husband, ashamed of her lack of control, hissed at her, 'Elspeth. Elspeth.'

When we began to enter our teens the high-spot of those yearly celebrations came to be occupied by a one-act play, performed by Glasgow-based nieces and nephews, produced by Aunt Evelyn, with Aunt Chrissie prepared to turn the drama into a star vehicle for herself.

About two weeks before Christmas, Aunt Evelyn would summon all potential players to a meeting. The play was her choice. It was always a comedy which, however it started out, became a farce as soon as it was staged before a live audience.

'Now children, you're to learn all your words,' Aunt Evelyn would say, having allocated parts. This was to be her repeated cry till the moment when the stage door in an alcove of the L-shaped drawing room swung open and the first actor made an entrance. As the days went on and the reality of the production took hold of them the temperature of Aunt Evelyn's exchanges with her recalcitrant cast rose steadily. One or two made no effort at all to be word-perfect on the night, relying on their ability to invent to pull them through, an attitude profoundly irritating to those who had laboriously memorised their parts and had no wish to find themselves at sea in a different scenario. In the middle of it all, as she intended to be in the centre of the stage, was Aunt Chrissie, reducing rehearsals to hysteria with her interpretation of her own character, never at a loss for suggestions for stage business, providing with a quick twitch of her clever fingers or a loan from her own wardrobe the touch that lifted a costume from the banal to the brilliant.

On the night the excitement engendered by the agony of expectation was almost unbearable. Bedrooms, stairs, landing were full of shrieks, laughter, bumps, stumblings, whispers. Aunt Evelyn, almost beside herself with nerves, the victim of a thousand calamities, distraught by the irresponsibility of those nominally under her direction, rushed from trouble-spot to trouble-spot attempting to restore a sense of order.

The audience, agog with anticipation and thoroughly enjoying these preliminaries, made helpful interjections to add to the confusion. Aunt Edith played a little music to keep us quiet. Aunt Lillias, a paper hat stuck jauntily over her bandeau, recalled previous Christmases, their highlights and disasters. Old Aunt Lucia had closed her good eye and was gently snoring. My mother demonstrated how to crack a walnut with her knuckles— her perennial Yuletide trick. Aunt Elspeth was already beginning to giggle.

The plays, when they at last began, were splendid. Familiarity bred hilarity and even the meekest member of the cast achieved heights of dramatic emphasis undreamed of in everyday life. In the middle of her nieces and nephews Aunt Chrissie, clutching bathrobe and sponge or mop and bucket, created a comic world uniquely her own.

After the Second World War, the parties, restarted by my eldest cousin, were not so hilarious, though no less enjoyable. There were gaps. The aunts, now the oldest generation, had themselves acquired great-nieces and nephews. Now it was our turn to produce the in-laws, to add the babies to the family tree. It may have been because my cousin's sitting room was smaller than those grand Victorian drawing-rooms, or perhaps the spreading branches of the tree really did shade more of us. Whatever the reason, in spite of losses, there seemed no diminution in the numbers.

We met at midday now, that being in those more straitened days a better time for ageing aunts and busy Mums with small new babies. It was a time which enabled Aunt Lillias to return to her essential image—in a hat. We sat down to lunch, thirty or forty of us, in two layers. Adults were in the dining room, young people in a basement playroom—an arrangement occasionally the cause of heart-burning among the junior members of the clan who did not always agree with the line of demarcation. Now we had sherry before lunch, the aunts abstaining, and afterwards there were no longer any special entertainments.

For an additional member—there by right of marriage rather than birth—the introduction into this new family was a formidable ordeal. First, the noise. Even out in the hall, or upstairs laying aside coats in the best bedroom, the froth of screams and laughter breaking over a roaring tide of sound could be heard from the sitting room.

This was the moment, before the plunge, when some hasty repairing of the grapevine could be undertaken in comparative calm. Once in the melee, verbal communication ceased to mean more than the tentative reaching-out of friendly kinship. Down there, in the tide race, any serious intelligence was conveyed by other means—observation, gesture, the mysterious telepathy which revealed, and understood, things rarely talked about.

The grapevine ran strongly through our own house, for my mother was a foundation member of it and took very seriously the job of keeping it watered and in good health. It was never certain whether the grapevine itself was an inanimate object, a web of family telegraph wires like those seen when a metal box in the road is opened up for work to be done, or whether it was a living plant, throwing out fresh tendrils in each generation, shrivelling if not watered with sufficient care, flourishing if judiciously tended, feeling pain if truncated, capable of stifling with its proliferating tendrils but leaving the world a more barren place if those tendrils failed to reach out far enough.

The information travelling round this invaluable circuit was usually factual, though often tinged with an interpretation which varied according to the branch that carried it. Occasionally a twig would burst into flower as a particularly juicy pint of sap pulsed through its veins. Letters were a vital fluid, and both my mother and Aunt Lillias were gifted letter writers. Malice was rarely an ingredient on the grapevine hot line. Criticism was usually oblique, but perfectly understood for all that.

Though it was enjoyable to be a natural member of such a network, this pleasure could be considerably mitigated if one became the object of its attention. Then the suspicion that opinions privately expressed, or actions which were no concern of anyone except those involved, were instantly widely-known and commented on was speedily confirmed. The result was fury and resentment and a vow to resort to a life of total secrecy. Ambivalent in my own mind, cherishing the titbits, appreciating the sense of family solidarity which knowledge conveyed, I yet grew cautiously selective about my contributions to the common stock. No one knew about that kiss on the aunts' doorstep. By that time I had learned to guard my tongue. Perhaps it is a paradox that, now that all the dedicated tenders of the grapevine are gone, I regret its demise. I feel my own nephews and nieces to be deprived. In a small, half shamefaced way I cherish the offshoot of grapevine that remains with me, giving it every now and then an enriching draught to help it take fresh root and flourish.

Newcomers were boosters to the grapevine. By the time of the Christmas party even those who had not managed to attend christening or wedding were in possession of details of physical appearance, likes and dislikes, opinions, prejudices, and the reactions of everyone concerned. The gathering set the seal on this sequel to acceptance and, in one devastating hour, introduced the bewildered incomers to their new-found relations.

When it was my turn I became conscious of how difficult it was to prepare an outsider adequately for the ordeal before him. A lifetime's intimacy, subtle, complex—loyal for the most part—heightened by the special memories of this occasion, made it impossible to impart the reality of each individual. The stereotyped phrases I seized upon described nothing of the truth. We knew too much about each other. In the end 'You'll see' became the extent of my advice.

Most relatives came to our wedding, but it had been a time of other preoccupations and almost immediately afterwards we had gone abroad. When my husband made his first entry to a Christmas party I saw a flicker of despair cross his face as he gallantly breasted the tide of relations, attempting vainly to provide himself with mnemonics to avoid offence. He had insisted on wearing a label giving his own name and attachment.

'This is Aunt Edith.' 'Here's Aunt Chrissie.' 'Hullo Aunt Gertrude, this is Alec.'

'What are their last names?' he would whisper.

'Sloan.'

'What, all of them?'

'And here's Aunt Gladys—and Uncle Tennant. Over there's Jenny, Wilfrid's wife, and David and Enid's three boys. Sloans—all Sloans.'

There were others, of course. Girls had married and changed their names. But on this occasion at least rebellion was stilled. In essence we all felt ourselves to be Sloans.

For two generations, and now briefly for a third, the corpus of unmarried sisters, the aunts, had been the cement of family solidarity. Because they appeared unalterable, and we the ones who developed and grew away, we could return with the easy confidence that here our past was still alive and the core of the relationship formed as children untouched. We took it for granted that they were on our side. We concealed from them, and for a brief time from ourselves, the things that had happened to us of which we felt that they might disapprove. We ignored the workings of the grapevine in this and discounted the resilience of human nature which the aunts too shared. Separately they could show themselves cognizant of life's troubles, and even our own failings, but together, at gatherings, we returned to our place in the family—nieces, nephews, cousins, who in this context were simply accepted for what we were.

It could, of course, be maddening too. There had been triumphs, challenges overcome, talents carefully trained, as well as sins committed and failures hidden. These too weighed very little in the balance when the family came together. There was a certain pride. The aunts would smile congratulations—sometimes getting vital details wrong. But these things were not what mattered in their eyes—or indeed at that moment in ours. The world could honour or disgrace us. What was important was that we belonged.

By this time, the late 1950s, the aunts had begun to move very gradually into old age. For thirty years, in the eyes of their nieces and nephews, they had hardly changed. Our perception of their physical appearance had been formed in those early days, when they had seemed so much older than they really were. As we grew up they tended to shrink, but each time we met, familiarity varnished the image on which a sharper gaze might have glimpsed the passing of time.

Nevertheless it was a long-lived family and some of them still had many years to go. It was a shock to realise that Aunt Chrissie's hair had gone grey, though under it her puckered, humorous face remained the same and her flair for startling garments undiminished. Aunt Lillias, now Miss Sloan, more hump-backed than ever but still in a lovat green suit and matching fur felt hat, took the armchair to the right of the fire and summoned to her those to whom she wished to speak. The cousin's husband had gone to fetch the sisters in a car, returning, when everyone had had time to get anxious, with a look of resignation on his face and Aunt Lillias and Aunt Chrissie still accusing each other of having been the cause of the delay—in both cases for the same reason, delicate decisions about clothes. Behind them came Aunt Evelyn, her expression clearly showing the shame her punctilious spirit felt at being the cause of concern and fuss, and little Aunt Gertrude, patient and calm.

It was impossible to imagine that the younger relatives thought of them as we had about the Old Aunts in Kersland Street. For one thing their dress was as up to date as our own, no sweeping black skirts or blouses caught at the throat by cameo. It would have shocked me, as an indication of my own advancing years, to have heard the rowdy great-nephews talk of the Old Aunts and mean a generation so near to my own. And yet I suppose neither Old Aunt Eliza with her 3D stereoscopic holder nor Aunt Lillias showing my own niece holiday snaps had thought themselves remote from modern life. Could it really be that Aunt Chrissie screaming with laughter at a ten-year-old's jokes aroused in him feelings comparable to our own when jaunty Old Aunt Mary stabbed a finger at us and shouted embarrassing questions across the room?

When everyone had arrived, a toast was drunk. It was always the same—Absent Friends. Of Agnes Paterson's six sons, only one now remained, and it was his duty to call the roll of those who were not able to be present. At those childhood parties Aunt Gertrude had been in India, as was her brother and his family. Aunt Nancy, with her husband and children, had lived in London, and Old Aunt Isabella was on the south coast. We were now a much more mobile generation. I had two brothers in Africa, and for some years had been an absent friend myself in that continent. There was a cousin in New Zealand, families in Cheshire and London, and increasingly the eyes of the young were to turn outward. The stability that had given the family cohesion, and enabled the aunts to remain at the centre of it, was dissolving. As communication became more rapid, we wrote to each other less fully and less frequently. The grapevine was breaking up into its component parts.

Then the newcomers were welcomed. The two-year-old shuffled behind Aunt Lillias's chair, to her manifest annoyance. The uneasy new husband or nervous bride fidgeted.

The dead we did not mention, but they were not forgotten. Each generation had its share of sorrow, and each knew it of the other and remembered—often in silence, though sometimes openly. In this kaleidoscope we enlarged our own experience. If we had a vision of the future, we also had a sense of the past.

8

Aunt Evelyn

Aunt Evelyn spent thirty-two years of her life as a substitute Mum. That at the end of this long period she returned of her own free will to share the communal menage with her sisters caused a good deal of astonishment among her nieces and nephews. She now had some financial security and could have made a separate home for herself. We did not consider that a joint household with one's sisters was at all the same in principle as the fashion, shortly to become widespread, for commune living, and we were surprised that Aunt Evelyn did not choose to go her own way.

All the aunts admired Aunt Evelyn's looks. My mother thought her beautiful and did not hesitate to say so to us—though I doubt if she ever told her sister her opinion. Certainly, until the day she died in her late eighties, Aunt Evelyn was a handsome woman, with an impeccable sense of dress.

She was tall, with a statuesque figure. It was her presence and personality that gave her the reputation for exceptional looks, for her face was irregular, pale-skinned, with the same puckish mouth as Aunt Chrissie and a 'Wellington' nose. She had humour and kindness and somewhere, well concealed from us all, immense reserves of self-control. But she was also nervy. The inner discipline took its toll in an occasional outward twitchiness. We made no connection between those two aspects, not realising until we ourselves were growing old the strains she must sometimes have lived under.

She was the twelfth child in the family, born in 1889 when her oldest brother was already eighteen and in business. With five senior sisters, and another baby shortly to supersede her, perhaps she learned early to keep her counsel and develop her own resources. To the little sister who followed her she showed a lifelong devotion. For both of them the departure for India of the brother immediately older than themselves was a great grief. At the end of his first leave, in September 1913, when he had just got engaged, Granny wrote; 'I was very sorry for Evelyn and Gertrude. They were very down and will miss you dreadfully...' adding, 'When you left last time they were scarcely able to appreciate the value of an older brother with them. Unfortunately these have an unfortunate way of getting other girls to care for them, and the sisters are left in the lurch.'

Aunt Evelyn was intelligent. She accompanied Aunt Chrissie to the new girls' school, Laurel Bank, which had been opened in 1903. From there she went on to Glasgow University. Of this latter achievement I, at least, remained unaware. Tradition related that the two girls drove to school in an open car with the number plate G2, sitting backwards. Whose car it was remains a mystery for their father never possessed one of his own.

There had been a close friendship between my father's family and the Sloans for many years, resulting in two marriages. At the beginning of the Great War Aunt Evelyn was on the high seas, a bridesmaid accompanying my father's sister travelling to India to marry the little boy who had once knocked her over. Whether they were genuinely chased by submarines or not, the retailing of nautical adventures later took an honourable place in the saga of reminiscence, as did the story of how the wedding ceremony in Naini Tal was interrupted by a guest who was forced to leave suddenly and felt that it was not polite to do so without first shaking hands with bride and groom—even if they were still before the altar.

After the marriage, Aunt Evelyn stayed on with her brother and new sister-in-law for some time. She followed the family sporting tradition and became Lady Golf Champion of Northern India. She took part in the active social life of the Indian Civil Service, and went on leisure trips to hunt game or seek the coolness of the hills. All this she greatly enjoyed, having the capacity to enter into other people's pleasures and interests with as much zest as though they had been her own. Somewhere, during this period, we were conscious, in the vague way that children pick ideas out of the atmosphere surrounding grown-up conversations, that there may have been a special young man. It was murmured that a young man in Scotland married while she was away. But these hints, this feeling, never became more than that and we gradually forgot that they had ever been present. After Aunt Evelyn died a photograph in a locket remained unidentified, and none of us ever knew the story that may have lain behind it.

She came back and went to work in a secretarial post in the Church Offices, and it was this that she was doing when, in 1919, her oldest brother's wife died, leaving four small children. The decision that one of the unmarried sisters should take over the job of keeping the family together was an obvious and sensible one.

There were five of them: Aunt Edith, forty-three that year, an able and accustomed housekeeper: Aunt Lillias, an invalid: Aunt Chrissie, still involved with post-war operations in Europe: Aunt Evelyn, working in a full-time paid position: and Aunt Gertrude, at the start of her nurse's training. It was not necessarily such an obvious decision when looked at from the personal point of view of any one of the sisters.

Uncle Norman had no hesitation. He wanted Aunt Evelyn. She agreed to go, but felt that she could not instantly throw up her commitment to her job. So, in the interim, Aunt Chrissie stepped into the breach. Her brief, haphazard reign only convinced her brother that his younger sister was the right one for the family.

For Aunt Evelyn there were practical problems. She knew nothing about running a house and found financial matters terrifying. Quite apart from the fact that girls in families who could afford servants had restricted contact with the actualities of household work, Aunt Evelyn herself came a long way down in the female hierarchy, so even management was a closed book to her. Some preparation was needed for the arduous life that lay immediately before her. She decided to take a course in domestic science at what was then known as the 'Dough School.'

Aunt Evelyn was thirty when this tragedy occurred and her whole life changed. Later we took the situation for granted, but it cannot have been a commitment that she entered into easily or lightly. In taking on the care of four children, who had already lost a mother through death, she must have deliberately put aside any thought of a future husband of her own. Both her older sisters had been in their thirties when they married, so such a possibility was by no means unthinkable. But it would not have been in her nature to accept a responsibility and then, within a year or two, to have renounced it for a personal advantage. None the less, never at any time were we given the least inkling that a sacrifice might have been made. On the contrary I often felt that she had managed to have the best of two worlds, to remain a single aunt, which had a number of selfish advantages for us, and yet to have acquired for herself an instant family.

For thirty-two years, with unswerving loyalty and rarely a cross word, Aunt Evelyn nurtured her brother and his children. She was punctilious about everyone arriving for meals on time and wearing their winter woollies. Bad manners and disrespect she would not tolerate. Her reprimands were sharp and brief—and always justified. She based her own life on a steadfast Christian faith, apparent by example to others but never preached. And she was always tremendous fun.

Like the rest of her family she enjoyed sports and the open air, and was addicted to Highland holidays. Not for nothing had she become Lady Golf Champion of Northern India. She shared with her sisters a love of bathing—even in the coldest mountain water. I remember my mother, on a day of high wind and storm, when her family cowered in a beach hut and her husband beseeched her to be more sensible, braving the waves of the Moray Firth, pretending—as we were all convinced—that she was enjoying it. So too Aunt Evelyn would be the first in and one of the last to come out, even in circumstances when her young charges had had second thoughts.

She shared the family enjoyment of travel. In her mid-sixties she made a solo journey across Scotland, from South Uist in the Outer Hebrides to Ballater on Deeside, the various stages of which gave ample fuel for subsequent anecdotes.

A car was hired from the hotel to the first sea crossing, made by horse and cart at half-tide. Safely over she caught a bus to the next ferry, this time a launch. Another bus transported her to the airport where she boarded an aeroplane to Inverness; next a train to Aberdeen, and again a bus to Ballater. This was one day's expedition and she arrived with energy undiminished, ready to recount to the sisters the minutiae of each encounter and to laugh with them over hazards negotiated, disasters narrowly averted, and impromptu conversations held in unlikely places.

In the 1950s her brother died. Aunt Evelyn had cared for her nephews and niece through good times and bad. She had watched them marry, come to terms with serious crippling illness, leave to fight a war, and produce children of their own.

She had been a foster mother, now she was a foster grandmother. During all this time she had never called herself other than Aunt Evelyn, though there must sometimes have been a temptation to distinguish her unique relationship with this family.

She came back at once, and without question, to share the home in Bute Gardens with her sisters. By now there were four of them, for Aunt Gertrude had retired from service in India, and the house was bulging. For no one, except herself, does this return to her original role appear to have been a foregone conclusion, though when it took place it quickly seemed as though she had never been away. The small room to the left of the front door became her bedroom. Questioned about her decision to go back she said; 'If four Christian women haven't the grace to live together it will be a pretty poor show.'

The physical constrictions and social constraints, after the spaciousness and privacy in which she had reigned supreme, must have been hard to bear. Harder still, perhaps, an aspect that went unrecognised. In a very real sense Aunt Evelyn was a widow; but the dignity of widowhood, even the comfort of widowhood, were denied her. She had shared her brother equally with her sisters, and the special bond which must have grown between them over those long years together was not acknowledged. It was his children to whom we all primarily gave our sympathy, and in the affairs that remained to be settled they took the responsibility. In a way which only she herself can have realised, and of which certainly only she knew the inward pain, Aunt Evelyn, who had steadfastly remained Aunt Evelyn, became again the unattached aunt that she had once been.

The first years back were not easy. There was evidence for this—though it was not admitted to be such. My mother used to talk of difficulties in settling down, of Aunt Evelyn being out more than was approved of, particularly in the evenings when there was occasionally a suggestion that she should have been at home to undertake certain duties. There were differences of opinion over church matters which went deep and caused much suffering. I would sometimes hear a veiled reference by Aunt Lillias to too much time spent in certain places or with certain people. The facial twitchiness, which had always been one of Aunt Evelyn's habits, increased.

Immersed in our own concerns, as the other aunts were immersed in theirs, we none of us considered how hard it was for Aunt Evelyn to readjust to the constant surveillance of family life, nor how unreasonable must have seemed to her the unspoken pressure to accept again group habits and customs of which she had long been free. There may have been secret moments when she regretted her decision.

If so she never spoke of such doubts. Always easy to talk to, conversations would often start with an expression of amazement at our doings, accompanied by incredulous laughter. In a curious way this humorous denial of involvement in our lives acted as a spur to tell her more, even to reveal matters which would not have been broached with other aunts, for the pleasure of hearing her exclaim our name in a manner that indicated enjoyment, astonishment and curiosity. She would screw up her face, sometimes with distaste, perhaps incomprehension, but never condemnation. Told a joke she would bubble with laughter and then cap it with an incident of her own.

Aunt Evelyn loved people and every facet of human behaviour interested her. Returning from what she called the 'bowels' of the city, where she had been quietly engaged in doing what she could to ameliorate dismal conditions and encourage spiritual growth, she would be full of anecdotes, sad, surprising or just silly; but in the telling of them it would quickly become clear how wide were her sympathies and how delicate her perceptions of the trials and temptations of her fellow human beings.

With young people Aunt Evelyn had a sure touch. Her own old school, where a niece was now the headmistress, backed on to Bute Gardens. When she returned to live there one of Aunt Evelyn's solaces was to work in the tiny flowering patch behind the house. In the school another niece taught in a classroom facing across the lane. When she saw Aunt Evelyn in the garden she would sometimes wave. One day, as Aunt Evelyn returned the signal, she said to her class of little girls, 'That's my auntie.' Delighted they turned to the big plate glass window, pink hands fluttering in salutation. Standing among the wallflowers, Aunt Evelyn smiled and gestured to her successors who, enjoying the break to smile at teacher's auntie, remained unaware that they were also looking at a founder-member of their school.

She liked to discuss the topics of the day with visiting nephews. One afternoon, when she was nearing her eighties, I discovered two young ministers-in-training enjoying tea and conversation with Aunt Evelyn. Immediately it was clear that they were not paying a duty visit on an old lady, but having a marvellous time and seeking advice about their work from someone whose judgment they respected. Not only their work: one of them came to consult her about his intended marriage, and was a friend until her death.

In the end it was Aunt Chrissie and Aunt Evelyn who were left alone together. In a small modern flat they retained the atmosphere that had always greeted us; a warm welcome telescoping time, paying no heed to our dilatoriness in visiting or the slow mutations of the years.

Superficially these two aunts were much alike in their zest for life and the ease with which they crossed the barriers of the generations, but in character they were very different. Uncushioned by numbers, the strain of living closely together, exacerbated by increasing age, took its toll. The burden fell most heavily upon Aunt Evelyn.

Though she sometimes gave the impression of being nervy and uncoordinated, Aunt Evelyn was a woman with considerable organisational and domestic skills. In her seventies and eighties she looked twenty years younger, continuing to be active and alert, with interests and friends outside her home. She was deeply involved in the affairs of her church—the same one in which her parents had been married and she herself christened— conducting classes for young people, acting as President of the Woman's Guild, supporting the minister, always ready when called on.

Aunt Chrissie, on the other hand, remained as scatty and impractical as she had been fifty years before when, for a brief while, she had reluctantly taken over her bereaved brother's household. But Aunt Chrissie was now Miss Sloan, and she still cared about the dignity of that position. When rate demands came in, or anything in a buff envelope that might have unpleasant financial implications, she hid them. This policy of masterly inaction resulted in great embarrassment for Aunt Evelyn, and in one or two comic situations. Aunt Chrissie, who put out of her mind such disturbing intrusions once she had dealt with them, was known to have written to the Lord Provost complaining of unjust harassment when a scarlet typed final demand fell through the letter box.

Gradually old age began to disorganise Aunt Chrissie's failing capacities. Memory became fickle, the lapses unacknowledged, or distressingly recognised. Traits which in her heyday had been part of her charm, forgiven her because they were an essential part of her ebullient personality, now became exaggerated and, in the inexorably narrowing circumference of her existence, a cause of strain. She was restless and demanding, as though her spirit remembered the days when she had been able to command her own life and did not understand why she could no longer do so. As her hold on existence had been strong and valiant, so now a battle raged within her to inhibit the recognition that she must let it go. She was not to be spared the full humiliation of physical dependence.

Yet, as deterioration progressed, so too did a merciful incomprehension. Forgetfulness can be a benediction. It was Aunt Evelyn, lovingly supported by the niece to whom she had been a second mother, who had to summon up faith and fortitude, and the capacity to endure; cutting off many of her outside activities and interests to watch over a sister whose slow metamorphosis must have been the cause of much pain. Nor is it easy always to sustain the tolerance which love and kinship dictate when one by one the ties of a lifelong association are being severed in preparation for a final leave-taking. The closer the intimacy, the more intertwined the common strands of memory, the greater the capacity for sudden anger or despair, the more grievous to the perpetrator the lapses in compassion.

To Aunt Evelyn it must often have seemed that her own life was being forcibly foreshortened. In her eighties, paradoxically, she had found something of the personal freedom that she had always willingly abandoned for the sake of others. It was a time to be selfish, but all she had been taught and learned, and all her actions since she was a young woman had made such a choice impossible. She came of a generation where death took place within the family. Going in to wake them in the early morning she had found both Aunt Edith and Aunt Lillias dead in their own beds. If she had the strength then Aunt Chrissie too would die in her own home.

Ultimately she did; and the grapevine hummed with plans for Aunt Evelyn, now for the first time alone. She did not need them. For the few years that she had left she could taste with a clear conscience and a light step the pleasures of independence. She grew younger, the gay Aunt Evelyn that we had always known, full of concern for our doings and gentle laughter, taking up again the activities within her church that she had had to lay aside. When death found her at last, in her eighty-ninth year, she went gladly and with no regrets.

9

Holidays

In our family a warm glow was cast over the relationship with the aunts simply by the fact that we generally met them when either we, or they, or perhaps both, were on holiday, undertaking a day's outing, or being given a treat. This arose mainly because we lived outside Glasgow. Nieces and nephews on their doorstep came into contact with them in more mundane situations, and knew the aunts on bad days as well as good in a way that we did not. There were moments, for all of us, when relatives seemed an unbearable burden and we wished that we had been found on the workhouse steps, but perhaps the surprising thing was the unanimity of our view of the aunts. I do not remember ever being disillusioned by whispered confidences in the rhododendron bushes when cousins came to stay—though some radical ideas about parents used occasionally to shock me, generally because, while secretly agreeing with them, I lacked the courage to voice them myself.

The fact was that parents bore the brunt of the rub and friction of everyday life in a way that, in our case, the aunts were not required to do. Vaguely aware that Aunt Edith might be strict, and continuous contact with Aunt Lillias a cause of frustrations, I was tolerant of their idiosyncracies because ultimately they had no power over my world. Indeed they presented an escape from it, greater in fantasy than in reality but none the less valuable. Though I never spoke to her of private hopes or fears, I was confident that Aunt Chrissie understood some of them. There was a strong, if quite unfounded, feeling that our affairs took priority over their own with the aunts and if a crisis arose they would, of course, come to the rescue. Growing up we talked about 'staying with the aunts' purely as a matter of our own convenience, as if they had no other life but to complement ours and disappeared when we chose to direct our eyes elsewhere.

A few years after the end of the Second War I asked Aunt Chrissie if she would like to come with myself, a friend and my mother on a holiday to Bruges in Belgium. The friend and I were both painters, as was Aunt Chrissie, but she and my mother were sisters, so it seemed a well balanced party.

She accepted with alacrity, and arrived in London dressed in yellow, brown and crimson clutching a variety of bags, practising her eccentric French at every opportunity. In this she outshone us all, having no self-consciousness about her own mistakes. My friend Nancy was enchanted by her. At Ostend, in the crowd of summer tourists, we got separated. When the huge transcontinental train slid into the platform at Bruges forty-five minutes later neither of them could be seen.

The stop was a short one; already the express was preparing itself for departure and doors were being slammed. I rushed wildly down the platform, certain in my own mind that we had left them at the port. Behind a fish tank window, convulsed with silent laughter, I suddenly spied our two missing companions, immersed in an entertaining conversation and quite unconscious of the need to disembark.

It annoyed me to see them enjoying themselves without a care in the world. It was irresponsible: it would serve them right if they were carried on into Europe. But I banged on the window all the same and, still laughing and quite unrepentant, they tumbled out just as the train pulled away. Neither my mother nor I was amused: I resented my friend commandeering my aunt, and my mother was horrified at the way we were all being made conspicuous.

She rapidly grew accustomed to this situation, however, and began to contribute her own share of public scenes. Free of the burden of kinship, my friend egged Aunt Chrissie on to wilder flights of enjoyable buffoonery, acting as stooge when necessary to her comic turns. It was I who felt betrayed, being presented for the first time, late in life, with visible evidence that Aunt Chrissie could exist in a dimension that did not necessarily revolve around her nieces and nephews.

Of course we knew this—but it was hearsay. In her presence we still considered that her attention should be centred on us. Other holidays on which we had been together were family affairs with the solidarity of the circle unbroken. If there had been strangers or unrelated friends present the subtle line of demarcation that separated kith from kin had remained clear. This time there was no such definition. Aunt Chrissie plainly liked my friend very much. She did not want constantly to be cast in the role of companion for an older, less agile sister and was not averse to going off alone with Nancy to look at sights in which both were interested. Though I resented it, I could think of no good reason why she should not.

One evening, walking leisurely after supper through brightly lit shopping streets, my mother and I in front, Aunt Chrissie and my friend behind, we heard them giggling before the window of a lingerie shop. Aunt Chrissie was pointing at an elegant built-up bra and indicating with sinuous gestures of her mobile hands what such an aid would do to her own flat chest. Then she called

out to me to come back and look and, laughing, said it was
exactly what I needed. I should buy one the next day.

It was a tremendous joke. Aunt Chrissie expounded on the
advantages for my skinny figure. My friend laughed; even my
mother, secure by now in her own handsome elderly bosom,
laughed. In the sharp contrasts of lights and darkness and the
casual hilarity perhaps they thought that I laughed too. But I did
not. Aunt Chrissie should have known. She might not mind, but I
did. In my dreams I had always longed to boast a bust like Miss
Hazeldene, the dancing teacher, down which I could drip endless
strings of pearls. Awake, even on the verge of thirty, the reality
still made me ashamed.

The *pension* was small and inexpensive, entered by an unpre-
possessing door off a narrow odorous side street. I had booked
belatedly and the rooms were the least comfortable. But Monsieur was charming. He clearly thought us a curious quartet.
Perhaps in his eyes Aunt Chrissie even added a touch of the
exotic.

She and my mother shared a bedroom under the roof. It was a
long thin coffin of a room, breathtakingly hot, and noisy. For both
of them sharing was an ordeal, made unbearable by the conditions in which they had to do it. Communal living was for the
daylight hours; the privacy of night-time infinitely precious.

The first morning, when they did not appear for breakfast, I
went up to see how they had slept. They were barely on speaking
terms. Aunt Chrissie was dithering round her end of the room in
a celanese slip, though there seemed no good reason why she
should not be already dressed. At the other end my mother, fully
clad, sat on the bed looking worn and harried. Both had had an
appalling night, lying sweating and sleepless, each unable to
indulge in her own particular panacea for such unfortunate
situations for fear that the other would be disturbed.

Now, determined not to venture downstairs alone, my mother
was doing her best to bring Aunt Chrissie to a state of readiness,

while Aunt Chrissie, unbearably irritated by this supervision, became more and more stubbornly confused. When I removed my mother, to her relief as well as Aunt Chrissie's, the latter quickly followed us having recovered her good humour and with it a determination to get the room changed.

This involved an approach to Monsieur, undertaken by me with apologetic diffidence. Aunt Chrissie, lurking in the wings, quickly intervened. Waving her hands, speaking rapid and very inaccurate French, to which he replied in broken but reasonable English, she charmed him into offering a better double room, on a lower floor, which to me he had denied being able to provide. For the rest of our stay Monsieur and Aunt Chrissie carried on an animated flirtation, the dimensions of which both perfectly understood. This produced in me the curious dilemma of occasionally wondering what the aunts would think, and then having to come to terms with the fact that it was one of them who was giving me reason to refer inwardly to their collective judgment. Having ineradicably imbibed the doctrine of personal inconspicuousness in my youth, I found it bewildering to discover that the aunts were capable of abandoning any such barrier to enjoyment when the occasion seemed to them to warrant it.

All their lives the aunts had been travellers and holiday-makers. Unlike the Old Aunts, they did not appear to us as static beings. Their background, thanks to the family chronicles, was wider than one house in one city. They were to be met with on hillsides, up remote glens, on ferry boats and steamers, by lochs and on beaches, and the continent or even India were not impossible auntly haunts. They were particularly addicted to old graveyards.

Once tried, and found acceptable, however, certain places became favourites and moving on always difficult. 'What a row we made the year we were told we were going to Strone,' (instead of Dalmally or Strathyre) my mother used to recall; or indeed when anything kept them from going to Moffat, or substituted Grantown-on-Spey for Ballater. I used sometimes to think that

Granny, faced with the united resistance to change that my
mother conjured up, must have had a difficult time negotiating
with her brood. Perhaps the need to reach a measure of agree-
ment among so many resulted in a reluctance to abandon any
place of general accord. In later years the sisters journeyed to
Cambus O' May, on Deeside in Aberdeenshire, and there, joined
by my mother, they continued to return annually until the last
holiday of their dwindling band.

Deeside held memories reaching far back for all of them. The
Cambus O' May Hotel and a railway halt on a one-track line were
eight or nine miles from the small town of Ballater where they had
spent many happy summers. It was at Ballater that Aunt Edith
had triumphed on the golf course and Grandfather had carved a
propeller for a small grandson and stuck it on his walking stick in
the river. Here, at the station, Aunt Lillias had watched the arrival
on holiday of countless royal parties and stored up details for
later dissemination. Balmoral was just up the road and Crathie,
where the minister was often known, a mile or two further on.
Banchory, where Aunt Lillias had spent the sick years of her
youth, lay in the other direction, and Aberdeen, which on a day's
excursion it was possible to reach by train.

Concentrated in those few miles of Highland territory were the
evocations of a corporate lifetime. Experiences undergone, the
remembrance of times past, of smells and sights and colours,
sporting triumphs or disasters, family joys and relations' rivalries,
though rightly belonging to other scenes were easily recalled by
the scent of a heather covered hillside, the splashing of a
mountain burn, the sight of a bicycle spinning down a gentle
slope, the sound of a soft accent in a village shop. And each year
fresh incidents joined those farther recollections, so that the
present was becoming the past even while the past was occupy-
ing the present, as writing on an unfinished scroll adds continual-
ly to the legend until the whole is unrolled for review.

The Cambus O' May Hotel was small and intimate, standing in
the shadow of a pine wood above the main road. The railway ran

parallel to the highway, and beyond it the river was crossed at this point by a gracefully suspended white footbridge which led into a stand of beech trees where, in the autumn, the colours burned and blazed. The hotel was seasonal. Each year the identity of the staff was a matter of great interest to the aunts. Once more it was Aunt Lillias who knew most about them, and looked forward to seeing again Mary, whose home was in the Outer Hebrides and who, in turn, remembered each one of her perennial guests and their weaknesses.

At first there were five sisters, known collectively as the Miss Sloans, though Mary was discreetly aware of the hierarchy and never treated it with disrespect—something that could not always be said for other, less sensitive, staff. Rooms were of great importance, and again it was Aunt Lillias who set the pace. She insisted, and no compromise was possible, on having the same room each summer, with the view and the washbasin that were both essential to her comfort. While Aunt Edith lived, recognition of the identity of Miss Sloan was not difficult and she also was allocated one of the better rooms. The younger aunts had to take their chance. Aunt Gertrude, the baby, was willing to accept quietly whatever she was given. So too was Aunt Evelyn who, though she might mutter in private, only made herself publicly conspicuous by accident and not intent. Aunt Chrissie was more unpredictable. Whether she felt outraged by being offered sec-ond-best depended on factors not necessarily controlled by the hotel. If she did, she had no hesitation in saying so.

It was Aunt Lillias, responsible for making the bookings specifying the exact rooms that she wished her sisters to have, who took up the cudgels on their behalf. 'Lillias!' Aunt Evelyn would hiss despairingly, seeing dudgeon loom on the horizon and the possibility of a scene; while Aunt Gertrude would be saying 'Evelyn!' in a tone of mild exasperation, indicating that she knew Aunt Lillias was not going to be deflected and and wished that Aunt Evelyn would stop adding to the incipient incident by trying to divert her.

Hiking, fishing, going by bus to Ballater, driving through the glorious countryside, attending local Highland Games were the relaxations of guests at Cambus O' May. The aunts were still good walkers. In tweeds and stout brogues with sticks, Aunt Edith, Aunt Evelyn and Aunt Gertrude would set off up the path through the pine wood and on to the hill behind, where curlews and peewits called, the beacon at the summit beckoned, and springy heather was glorious with shades of madder, purple and mauve. A constant watch was kept for the clump of white which would provide souvenirs, and perhaps also luck. But roots of the humble ordinary purple would also go back to Glasgow, to be cherished through the winter as a reminder of past beauties and a promise of future pleasures. Each one of their bedside Bibles held its sprig of ling, faded and flattened but still emitting the faint sweet scent that could trigger off so many memories.

Meanwhile Aunt Chrissie, in a battered but still elegant straw hat, a chiffon scarf wound round her skinny throat, sketched on a rock by the river or among the rusty drying bracken at the edge of the beech wood, her volatile temperament disciplined by the claims of her art. She worked in water colour, with a sureness of touch, a delicacy of tint and an inward control that belied her often chaotic outward impression. In a canvas chair on the grass in front of the hotel Aunt Lillias, keeping herself informed of what was happening in the world she had left behind, sat in the sun reading the daily paper which Aunt Evelyn collected off the van at the gate every morning.

Not far away, in a rather larger hotel, their brother and his wife would be accommodated. They had a car and, although it was not possible to take all of them at the same time, the brother enjoyed acting as chauffeur to his sisters. The small squabbles that took place over who should go, when an expedition was being planned, the exclamations of self-sacrifice, the suggestions as to route—which could end in an adviser who was not to be one of the party being told that if they knew so much about it they had better go after all—were part and parcel of leisurely enjoyment.

Each sister prided herself on her geographical knowledge of the area, and each knew better than any of the others where the best picnic places were, what distances were involved and the state of the roads. Only Aunt Gertrude would be willing to haul down her colours and retire from the battle before she had convinced everyone else that her own views were the rational ones. For the rest, up to the moment of departure the contest for domination of the afternoon's excursion raged; and for those who actually undertook it nothing short of the return home solved the argument about who knew best.

So the family passion for picnics could be fully indulged—in rather more comfort than formerly with folding table and chairs. A certain amount of discreet royalty-watching, even the excitement of seeing the Queen Mother's party on a stalk above Loch Muick, fishing, sketching, walking beside the Linn of Dee, attending Sunday morning service at Crathie Church, year after year these things formed part of the landscape of relaxation that bound them together.

The more active might sometimes take a bus into Ballater or have the station-master flag down the train, and once in the village comb the streets for remembered corners, make pretexts to go into shops so as to discover whether the original owners— from the twenties and thirties, or even earlier—were still in command, and if so to enter into a prolonged, delightful five minutes of reminiscence until a murmur of protest from behind made it clear that almost half an hour had passed. There was the station to be visited, where a number of monarchs had been glimpsed, perhaps even a corner of a road to haunt on the rumour that a royal car might flash by; and for the more energetic, past triumphs on the golf course could be relived hole by hole, though now in memory only.

In the hotel itself the Miss Sloans were by no means the only visitors who, like migrating birds, were drawn back by a pull the strength of which it was not always easy to account for. Certainly Aunt Lillias, less able to explore than the others, found those summer friends an attraction. Their tales of winter months spent in London, Jersey or Edinburgh were grist to her alert interest in the details of other people's lives, and they added an extra dimension to the daily orchestration of comings and goings in the hotel itself, the food, difficulties in the kitchen, cold water or hot water, who wanted which programme on the television, the weather, changes that had taken place or were threatened in the future.

Sometimes these topics were a cause of dissension, though never seriously. The fact that one of the annual visitors was stone deaf made for an embarrassing degree of very public comment, in which genuine warmth of feeling towards one so cut off from normal conversation wrestled with an equally genuine dislike in the aunts of appearing to be over-conspicuous. But when, as the years went by, the clientele began subtly to alter, the occasional bus party to appear for a meal, differences among those who now felt that the hotel had come to belong to them vanished and, abandoning the main public room to the hoi polloi, they would all retire, with a slight visible huffiness, to a small side lounge or, in extreme cases, to their bedrooms.

Aunt Edith was the first to die. My mother remarked, with some satisfaction at the fitness of nature, 'It's as it should be. We're going in the right order.' She was to be proved wrong before long. Quiet Aunt Gertrude was the next to go, and my mother, herself the eighth-born, was destined to outlive them all.

The summer visits to Cambus O' May continued and were enjoyed. Death was not only the inevitable end to life, it was also a fitting climax, a time for the testing of their faith, and they did not shrink from it.

As age, almost imperceptibly, crept up on those who remained, so the radius of their activities contracted. The objectives of hill walks were less distant from the hotel. A stroll in the scented pine wood or down over the suspension bridge and through the crimsoning beech trees came to seem normal for a morning's exercise. Aunt Chrissie ceased to sketch, though her appreciation of a view or the composition of tree and water remained undimmed, now expressed only by an eloquent gesture. She fell and broke a leg on an uneven step in the middle of a narrow corridor, and the hazards of the hotel's physical layout, which had never been so apparent before, were suddenly noticeable. Taken into Aberdeen her dentures disappeared between Cambus O' May and the hospital, causing such hilarious confusion that the original disaster was completely overshadowed. It took several days before they were discovered in the bottom of her handbag.

The ability to command a car ceased when their brother decided to spend his summers elsewhere, though an affluent cousin living near at hand provided hers for an exceptional outing. The railway line was closed; grass began to veil the track and the hard concrete of the platform at the halt proved to be clay to the tendrils of returning plants. The bus service to Ballater, once so convenient, still ran, but times no longer fitted the declining energies of the aunts.

There were rumours of a change of management. One year Mary did not come back. The lounge was filled with fishing men, and transitory young couples who laughed and joked, took out huge packed lunches and in the evening argued over television programmes. They could not know that the Miss Sloans were an institution and treated the hotel as though it were their own. The new waitress put plates of man-sized portions down before Aunt Lillias, uninterested in her fastidious appetite. In the daily paper the column of deaths became the most compelling reading. The deaf friend from London lost whatever residual hearing she may once have had and conversation with her sank to a trickle, helped out by nods and smiles.

Outside, the landscape remained unchanged. Extra holiday traffic on the road was invisible from the top of the sloping grass lawn where Aunt Lillias sat. Across the silent railway line the beech wood spread its branches over the thickening autumn mast and the suspension bridge swung slightly in the breeze as it had always done. On the hill behind the dark green pine trees the occasional grouse rose with a whirr; the sky was as blue as it had ever been, the rowan berries as red, and the swallows sitting along the telegraph wires before the long flight south would certainly be back again next year.

I tried to persuade my mother, and through her the aunts, to make a change. It seemed so obvious that they would all benefit from a move to a hotel in the village itself, where shops were close at hand and a morning's stroll would be easy and full of interest. They murmured acquiescence to my arguments, but already they had passed beyond the possibility of such an upheaval. It involved, on however small a scale, the making of a fresh start. If the hotel at Cambus O' May had been burnt down the effort might have been happily achieved, but as a spontaneous initiative it was no longer possible. Where once they had planned ahead with eager anticipation, now the sisters were content to accept quietly what was already there. Individually Aunt Evelyn and Aunt Chrissie still went to stay with friends but for the group the spring had broken. One year, through illness and hesitation, no bookings were made. That summer and autumn Deeside went about its usual business without a Sloan presence in the wings.

10

Aunt Gertrude

Her oldest brother was twenty when Aunt Gertrude was born in 1891. She was two years younger than Aunt Evelyn and five years Aunt Chrissie's junior, the last of the long line of high-spirited, strong-minded, clearly differentiated offspring of Agnes Paterson and Alexander Sloan. In her own way Aunt Gertrude too inherited the family characteristics.

Coming at the end she might very well have been over-whelmed. Granny was only forty-four, but she had had twenty years of recurring pregnancies. Six older sisters, to whom yet another addition to the family was a commonplace event, could have resulted in a small girl oppressed by her position, alternately bullied or ignored by the others, nervous and anxious to please with little mind of her own. Perhaps she was saved by the very size of the family, which in itself spread tensions and stresses and ensured that there was always encouragement to be had from one source or another. Aunt Edith, at fifteen, was ready to feel responsible for the new baby. Aunt Evelyn, aged two, became and remained devoted to her. The core of affection which bound them all so strongly together included automatically this new addition.

Grandfather was delighted with his youngest daughter and grew very close to her. In an age when there was no artificial control of conception, neither was there any question of guilt or anger at a 'mistake', or unease about social disapproval. Without a choice, necessity made for acceptance and adaptability; faith bred confidence. In this family each birth brought a gift from God, who was welcomed and cherished as such. It would have been unthinkable that another child could be the occasion for regret at loss of personal opportunities, or unwanted in the sense of being actively unsought.

As we knew her Aunt Gertrude was quiet. She was round and small, with a full-cheeked brown face, brown eyes, brown hair and a tucked-in mouth. After all she may have found it expedient to keep her own counsel as she grew up. She was more likely to be confided in than to relate confidences of her own, and this very peacefulness made her easily approachable. She could be relied upon to remain calm whatever happened. Perhaps it was this quality, among others, which made Granny call her, when writing to her, 'My best little daughter.' In the shrill ferment of the Bute Gardens tea parties Aunt Gertrude's voice was rarely dominant. Indeed at those functions it was her role to sit at the table in the window dispensing tea from the silver pot into thin china cups.

Her older sister, Nancy, left for India, a qualified missionary doctor, when Aunt Gertrude was about twelve. Perhaps it was not surprising that Aunt Gertrude herself should decide to become a nurse. She took her training in the Western Infirmary, Glasgow, gaining a medal for outstanding work, and went on to complete her midwifery course in Edinburgh. She then settled down to a nursing career. She was thirty-two when, in 1923,

Grandfather became alert to the fact that she too wished to 'offer for India.'

Granny was in poor health and Grandfather, whose primary concern had always been for his wife, wrote to his youngest daughter to say that 'however his heartstrings might be wrung' he would gladly let her follow God's will, but that because her mother was in a precarious state he feared that 'any announcement of such a nature might be somewhat prejudicial to her.' He suggested that he consult Aunt Edith and perhaps it would be possible to make some kind of conditional offer, the fulfilment of which might depend on Granny's recovery. Two generations later it seems strange to think that, with three unmarried daughters living at home, there should have been any question of Aunt Gertrude not following her vocation. But this was her greatly loved youngest daughter, and it may be that Grandfather sensed that Granny was approaching the end.

She died that same year. After an interval Aunt Gertrude made her offer and sailed for India in the autumn of 1925.

Before she left she acted as bridesmaid at the wedding of her remaining unmarried brother, who came to matrimony late in life. Aged seven, I was a flower girl to the bride—many years younger than her groom. The confusion of generations on this occasion altered my perspective of Aunt Gertrude who, till that day, had appeared to inhabit the same unsignposted stretch of middle age as the other aunts. To find her standing alongside myself, in a role which experience so far had led me to believe belonged solely to those whom I knew to be young, jolted my perception of her. I had seen photographs of Aunt Gertrude, with some of her sisters, as bridesmaids at my mother's wedding, an event so far lost in the mists of time that it must then have been an entirely proper function for any aunt to undertake. Now, in her ceremonial finery, I really looked at Aunt Gertrude for the first time and saw that she was not as old as I had imagined. This realisation gave her a certain distinction, marking her out from the other aunts. Where their youth was a matter of well-recorded history, for an instant I had glimpsed hers for myself.

From the moment that Aunt Gertrude left for India until he died two years later Grandfather wrote to her regularly once a fortnight. She was appointed to the Church of Scotland hospital at Poona, a few hours from Bombay, and served there as sister, and then as matron, for twenty-five years. In 1946 she was joined by a niece who had graduated as a doctor and who, when she retired in 1978, had completed a century of missionary work in India, passing in line from aunt to niece, since Old Aunt Tina first arrived in Bombay in 1878.

In her working life Aunt Gertrude showed many of the strong Sloan characteristics that were muted in her in the family setting at home. She was a strict disciplinarian, but her young Indian nurses loved her and had no hesitation in coming to her for advice and help. There were hospital jokes, however, about her footwear. She was said to favour soft-soled shoes so that her arrival went unheralded. When the clack of her tread rang through the wards, then everyone knew that Matron was off-duty and going out. Forthright, fearless and honest, the whole mission knew where she stood and respected her views. She built up a nursing training programme that became accepted as a standard of excellence all over India.

When her young niece arrived to fill a senior medical post, Aunt Gertrude was on leave. On her return she attempted to hold on to some remnant of the hierarchical view of life which pertained in Glasgow. After all, in India, she was Miss Sloan. The niece, however, perceived the relationship between two professional women in somewhat different terms and insisted on dropping the otherwise obligatory 'aunt'. She succeeded, but to the amusement of them both Matron began occasionally to be referred to by other colleagues as 'Aunt G.'

Perhaps it was not surprising, with this strong strand of missionary endeavour running through three generations of the family, that I sometimes felt a moral imperative to join them. It was an internal pressure, secretly anguishing, silently argued, for I guessed that my mother would have greeted such a declaration of intent with opposition and alarm. Ultimately she would have become resigned, but before that state was reached she would have resorted to endless subtle stratagems, which I was ill-equipped to withstand, to make me change my mind.

Though haunted by a conscience which bade me go, my natural inclination, for different reasons, ran parallel with my mother's imagined opposition and this in turn complicated still further my nightly soul-searching, for I also felt that cowardice and parental dismay were unworthy reasons for refusing to engage in a higher cause. How fortunate it was for my peace of mind that Aunt Chrissie with her joyful artist's alternative began to impinge more and more upon my consciousness at this time.

Every five years Aunt Gertrude came home on leave. Her ship docked in the south and she took the train to Scotland. The main railway line ran through Beattock station. Going north the train stopped for a few moments to take on water, and perhaps to add an extra engine for the long climb up the summit. We stood on the platform, anxiously eyeing the interminable length of the express as it stretched out along the rail to a glittering point in infinity, watching for a small brown face to poke out looking, in its turn, for us.

Unable to contain themselves for excitement, not at the return of an aunt from foreign parts but at the breath-taking spectacle of the great steel leviathan snorting gently in its pride, dwarfing our minor station as it drew slowly to a standstill, my young brothers tore up and down the platform admiring it. Convinced that it was themselves who would first see Aunt Gertrude, they had in reality eyes for nothing except the train and were always surprised to find that she had appeared and was chatting at a carriage door while they were still staring fascinated at the guard. This was a joyous reunion, although the words said were of the most banal and few of them were ours. There was a sharp scent of romance in this encounter. For the boys the train might be the focus of attention, for me it was 'wee Aunt Gertrude', as my mother always called her.

Tiny in comparison to the monster that encased her, brown in a way that no amount of Scottish sunbathing ever achieved, I felt that she had come straight from India on this very train. I would not have been too surprised to find it filled with women in saris, camels and oxen, and several of the little dark babies that she had brought into the world, still in some mysterious way unable to dissociate themselves from her.

Each time she saw us afresh after a long absence she must have found us greatly changed. I was seven when she went to India, and twelve when she first came back. She looked at us and exclaimed at our height, our hair, our learning, all the visible alterations. But to me Aunt Gertrude always looked the same. I never noticed, till my mother said so, whether she was well or ill, plump or thin, showing her age or looking young. What was astonishing in my eyes was that, coming from a country infinitely different and distant and from experiences which my imagination found fearful, she should remain so extraordinarily the same.

She always brought us presents and sometimes, if we were all well organised, she would give them to us there on the station platform: little carved and painted wooden figures—a woman with a water pot, an ox cart drawn by oxen, a thin man in a dhoti with a stick, and many more. These were the people I would not have been surprised to see with her on the train. Once she brought me a beautiful pink sari; sometimes, when I grew older, pieces of rich patterned Indian silk.

Perhaps it was those gifts, seeming to show an understanding of pleasure in personal adornment which her own appearance would otherwise never have indicated, that made me buy earrings with her twenty-first birthday gift. Small turquoises dropping on silver chains, I found them in an antique shop in Edinburgh. They were the first earrings I had ever possessed and

I was ravished by them. I have them still and have always thought of them as Aunt Gertrude's earrings.

But when I showed them to my mother she was upset. She thought them frivolous, not worthy of the earnest efforts that 'wee Aunt Gertrude' had put into earning the money that went to pay for them. Perhaps she was right. I never asked Aunt Gertrude, preferring to cherish the illusion planted in me by the pink and gold sari and the gorgeous glowing silks that she would not have been displeased.

The return journey to the East had a different character. This time the express did not stop at Beattock, but roared through at high speed. Half a mile south of the station the line ran along a raised embankment through flat fields. The road lay parallel to it for several hundred yards, but at sufficient distance to make it possible for anyone standing in the train to keep in view for a short while a watcher on the highway.

We parked the car on the verge at least fifteen minutes before the train was due, and I have no doubt that Aunt Gertrude took up her place at the window at about the same moment. In my mother's family to be on time was to be early. Then we sorted out the clean handkerchiefs or scarves brought with us and searched for any bump in the ground that would give an extra advantage in height.

It could be a beautiful sunny day, with the larks calling in an azure sky. My mother would say, 'She's getting a lovely day to go. She'll remember it like this.' Or it might be cold and blustery, with melancholy grey clouds massed on the horizon over England. Then my mother would say, 'It's good to leave on a bad day. You don't mind so much.'

We cocked our ears for the distant throbbing and grew nervous with the fear that after all we should not see her. Then the rails began to sing and away to the north, beyond the houses of the village, a noise like rising thunder could be heard. Clutching our handkerchiefs, our throats dry with the anticipation of sadness, we prepared to wave. With lacerating suddenness the train burst out into the open space and for six or seven seconds hung there in front of us while we shouted to each other, 'Can you see her?' 'Is she there?'

Then it was gone, drumming away into the distance towards England, India and the ocean in between. But we had seen her. She was always there. A small blurred figure standing in the corridor, waving frantically towards the spot where she knew with absolute certainty that we would be whether, through the veil of her emotion, we were visible to her or not.

Turning to go home we were fully aware of the magnitude of the adventure this small, dumpy aunt was undertaking. For us five years was almost unimaginable. Nobody said, 'It won't be long before she's back.' It would be a different world when she was due once more to halt at Beattock station.

The train, rushing and rocking towards the south, where the rails met in a pinpoint of distant light, was always a source of thrilling excitement. How much more so when we knew someone on it. It would cross the border into England, a country both familiar and strange, and draw into London, a city fearful and attractive owing something of its image to John Bunyan's Vanity Fair. Then our aunt would go on board a ship and set sail for exotic oceans, accompanied by dolphins and flying fish, through the Red Sea which Moses had divided to the land of women carrying water pots and newly-born brown babies.

As the days drew out into weeks we might look at a map and say, 'Now she's there—or there—or there'; and the sense of time and distance, and the strangeness involved in this journey, became tangible, full of weight and colour, in a way that stretched the horizons of our understanding. When it was so much travail to get there, we had no doubt that India must be where Aunt Gertrude's real life lay.

But of course this was not entirely true and in the early 1950s she finally came home. Once again time played tricks with our perceptions and before many months it seemed as though Aunt Gertrude had always been one of the group of aunts living at Bute Gardens.

For her it must have been different. Once, when I had been very young, I had for an instant seen Aunt Gertrude as someone other than simply my aunt; now the gap in understanding might have narrowed but I was preoccupied with experiences of my own and she had returned to the accepted pattern of aunts. Indeed she slid into the niche that awaited her so easily, with so little fuss, that perhaps only one of us—the niece whom she had left behind in India with whom she kept up an intimate correspondence—realised how difficult it must sometimes have been, or how great was the contrast with her other life where she had possessed authority and earned honour and affection.

It was in her nature to be quiet and she took her position in the hierarchy as though the intervening years had made no difference—which indeed they had not. She was expected to conform to the rules of the household and publicly rebuked when, for whatever reason, she did not. Accustomed to the exercise of tact when faced with the discrimination of a medical establishment, she was equally discreet in the world of her sisters. She was still the youngest; she had come also to be the one on whom the others could lean. In that ebullient house her reticence, the quality of self-effacement which had nothing to do with lack of character, her concern for the needs of others, suited her for the role of safety valve. She was a buffer when exasperation surfaced, a confidante when personal problems loomed large. In her case the grapevine went no further.

She made her last family appearance at a Christmas gathering. She was the only sister of whom it could be said that she died before old age had begun to close in. Already in pain from cancer, though we still thought it to be the lingering result of shingles, she sat on a sofa surrounded by young relatives, laughing with them as she had always done. Only to the Indian niece had she revealed her own hopes and fears, with a request that there be no answering comment which might be read by others. Being a nurse she must have herself suspected the truth: being Aunt Gertrude she would never have let it overshadow the enjoyment of the family.

11

Epilogue

We had six other, married, aunts besides uncles and innumerable cousins and second cousins. Because we were born into this extensive network of relations we took for granted the richness and variety of our tribal connection. It had its disadvantages—as had living in a village, where privacy was suspect and the postmistress sometimes aware of celebration or catastrophe in our family before we were ourselves. The frustrations of being known to so many could be shattering at times when the public image seemed especially out of focus with an inward conviction of uniqueness. The knowledge that we were discussed in a context wider than our own home, and measured against universal standards, could be onerous on bad days when stories of that other far-off youth contributed to a sense of inadequacy. Anyway, had we not heard it all before?

There were pressures to conform, but as so often they came

more from within than without. Imagined strictures were powerful: tentatively tested they could prove to be chimera. There were
enough patterns to breed tolerance. One thing at least was
certain. We had a place. We knew who we were. Extreme
deviation would cause sorrow, but it would not alter the quality of
the affection.

It was the unmarried aunts who embodied the heart of the
family. Where other relatives had clearly defined lives of their
own, and personal relationships to which they gave priority, The
Aunts were ubiquitous. When we were with them *we* were the
ones who mattered. We could be mobile; in their group manifes-
tation they were stable. Though physical continuity lay with us, it
was they who cherished the family history and showed us what
kind of stock we sprang from. Men make family trees and fill in
lines of lineage on them: it is the women who give life and vitality
to those lists of names and dates. Cousin Maud's beauty and the
tales of the young men who sought to possess it, great-grandfather's bankruptcy and its effect on his daughters, the eccentricities
of an Irish uncle-in-law, the strengths and weaknesses, foibles
and heroisms of the multitude whose blood we shared, were
retold through the generations by the women.

There were many kinds of precedents and, like my mother's
need to find facial resemblances within the known connection for
any stranger newly met, some could be tiresome. To be rem-
inded that one was a throwback to Grandfather's sister Great-
aunt Maggie, when all one wanted was personal recognition for
an achievement or quiet oblivion for a gaffe, was sometimes hard
to stomach. Equally so the astonished comment, 'I don't know
where you got that from!' as though the virtuosity just displayed
had no validity unless its ancestry could be traced. But though we
may have rebelled, there was the sense of being an essential motif
within a grand design, an individual unit enriched by the reflec-
tions and echoes of the greater whole.

The aunts were maiden aunts, but they fitted none of the
categories into which such spinsters were cast in Victorian

stories. Unmarried ladies they might be, but I never thought them ignorant. Sometimes I feared to shock them—because certain things they did not talk about, not because they lacked understanding. Perhaps there was wisdom in their reticence.

For every generation theirs is a time of change and we were no exception. The aunts flung a bridgehead across potential chasms. It was a great advantage that they could be ignored between visits, without guilt on our part or umbrage on theirs. We all knew that when we returned they would greet us as they had always done, providing a temporary refuge from outside troubles and responsibilities. With them we could laugh—and relax enough to admire their values. Changeless, but never fossilised, they kept the world stable.

They belonged to a generation that did not find it easy to talk to nieces and nephews of deeply-held beliefs, though paradoxically they never shrank from revealing their Christian faith to young people in the context of the church. We did not expect them to solve the complex problems of adolescence or to answer questions which we would have had difficulty in framing. Their role was a different one; with them we could often be more nearly the kind of person we thought ourselves to be, because the traumas of revelation were absent in our relationship. The term 'Aunt' was a bond not a barrier, a sign that, whatever they might be to other people, they had a particular and prized link with us.

We did not have to ask what the aunts stood for—or to be told. Everything that we knew about them—and observed—made plain the foundations of their lives. Occasionally I spent a night alone at Bute Gardens when the bustle and gaiety of family visits were laid aside. Then I saw something of the art, and beneath it the effort, that went into the maintenance of domestic peace. They were not meek women, their quirks of character ironed out by youthful repression. On the contrary family life had taught them to be competitive and developed strong instincts for self-survival. None of them found it always easy to give way graciously, to tread with care on another's dreams and prejudices, to cultivate patience in the face of a cherished foible. That they were of one blood and loved each other did not necessarily make it simpler, for each must have been aware that the others guessed something of her secret thoughts and there was no escape from old memories of youthful blunders. But they had learned how to make allowances. In her own way each cultivated an inner life of courage, prayer and self-discipline.

We remained largely unheeding of the lives they lived outside their home—though expecting that they would take an interest in our non-family concerns. Perhaps they felt frustrated at this failure in us to recognise the importance of aspects of their existence unconnected with being aunts. If so they never showed it. They had learned that relationships were precious and to be cherished in their own right and on their own terms.

It was only late in life that I began to recognise the value of lessons learnt from the aunts, or indeed to realise that there were lessons learned at all. A variety of pressures, and in two cases deliberate choice, kept them together. They made an art of this communal life. Trials were faced with cheerfulness; loving-kindness never failed. They were too strong-minded for us not to be aware that they were human. Unlike the patient portraits of more remote ancestors, the aunts did not inhabit a different world.

In old age the fact that they were unmarried ceased to have any significance. They were not afraid of death, knowing themselves surrounded by the great cloud of witnesses who had gone before.

Aunt Evelyn was the last to die. On a beautiful spring day her funeral took place in the church in which her parents and both her sisters had been married and she herself had been christened, and to which until a few weeks before her death she had given such devoted service. She was eighty-nine. It was astonishing to see in the congregation so many middle-aged and young people from outside the family.

Afterwards we went for tea in the small bright flat which had been Aunt Chrissie and Aunt Evelyn's home towards the end of their lives. We were all there, the nieces and nephews, great-nieces and great-nephews, and the three remaining matriarchs in their nineties, my mother the last of her family, and her two sisters-in-law.

It could well have been a melancholy occasion—but it was not, though it seemed possible that, with the core of the family gone, it might be the last gathering. Leaving the church my mother, in her confusion, on being told that we were going to tea at the flat said; 'Will Aunt Evelyn be there?' In a sense she was, they all were, as looking at each other we renewed the family solidarity and remembered again life with the aunts.

Thomas Paterson m Janet Scott

Helen William Lillias JENTY MARY TINA Cassi

AGNES
m
Alexander Sloan

Norman Tom Willie Alec EDITH Nancy LILLIAS Mora
m ＼＿／ m m m
Edith died young Elspeth Graham Lauren